Aging
in
Rural
Canada

by

Norah Christine Keating, Ph.D.

Professor, Department of Family Studies
University of Alberta

Aging in Rural Canada
© Butterworths Canada Ltd. 1991

Printed and bound in Canada by John Deyell Company

The Butterworth Group of Companies

Canada:	Butterworths Canada Ltd., Toronto and Vancouver, 75 Clegg Road, Markham, Ontario, L6G 1A1 and 409 Granville St., Ste. 1455, Vancouver, B.C., V6C 1T2
Australia	Butterworths Pty Ltd., Sydney, Melbourne, Brisbane, Adelaide, Perth, Canberra and Hobart
Ireland	Butterworths (Ireland) Ltd., Dublin
New Zealand	Butterworths of New Zealand Ltd., Wellington and Auckland
Puerto Rico	Equity de Puerto Rico, Inc., Hato Rey
Singapore	Malayan Law Journal Pte. Ltd., Singapore
United Kingdom	Butterworth & Co. (Publishers) Ltd., London and Edinburgh
United States	Butterworth Legal Publishers, Austin, Texas; Boston, Massachusetts; Clearwater, Florida (D & S Publishers); Orford, New Hampshire (Equity Publishing); St. Paul, Minnesota; and Seattle, Washington

Canadian Cataloguing in Publication Data

Keating, Norah Christine
    Aging in Rural Canada

(Butterworths perspectives on individual and population aging series)
Includes bibliographical references and index.
ISBN 0-409-88855-9

1. Aged - Canada.   2. Canada - Rural conditions.
I. Title.   II. Series: Perspectives on individual
and population aging.

HQ1064.C3K4 1991   305.26'0971   C91-094097-5

Sponsoring Editors - Gloria Vitale and Sandra Magico
Developmental Editor - Ed O'Connor
Editor - Agatha Cinader
Cover Design - Patrick Ng
Production - Kevin Skinner

To my good friends in Summerland, British Columbia
who talked to me about their experiences
of aging in rural Canada
and encouraged me throughout this project

and

To my parents, Ruth and Bill Keating
whose retirement first raised my interest
in the process of aging
and who provided the urban foil for this
rural endeavour

BUTTERWORTHS PERSPECTIVES ON INDIVIDUAL AND POPULATION AGING SERIES

This Series represents an exciting and significant development for the field of gerontology in Canada. The production of the Canadian-based knowledge about individual and population aging is expanding rapidly, and students, scholars and practitioners are seeking comprehensive yet succinct summaries of the literature on specific topics. Recognizing the common need of this diverse community of gerontologists, Janet Turner, while she was Sponsoring Editor at Butterworths, conceived the idea of a series of specialized monographs that could be used in gerontology courses to complement existing texts and, at the same time, to serve as a valuable reference for those initiating research, developing policies, or providing services to elderly Canadians.

Each monograph includes a state-of-the-art review and analysis of the Canadian-based scientific and professional knowledge on the topic. Where appropriate for comparative purposes, information from other countries is introduced. In addition, some important policy and program implications of the current knowledge base are discussed, and unanswered policy and research questions are raised to stimulate further work in the area. The monographs are written for a wide audience: undergraduate students in a variety of gerontology courses; graduate students and research personnel who need a summary and analysis of the Canadian literature prior to initiating research projects; practitioners who are involved in the daily planning and delivery of services to aging adults; and policy-makers who require current and reliable information in order to design, implement and evaluate policies and legislation for an aging population.

The decision to publish a monograph on a specific topic is based in part on the relevance of the topic for the academic and professional community, as well as on the amount of information available at the time an author is signed to a contract. Because gerontology in Canada is attracting large numbers of highly qualified graduate students as well as increasingly active research personnel in academic, public and private settings, new areas of concentrated research are evolving. Future monographs will reflect this evolution of knowledge pertaining to individual or population aging in Canada.

Before introducing the fourteenth monograph in the Series, I would like, on behalf of the Series' authors and the gerontology community, to acknowledge the following members of the Butterworths "team" and their respective staff for their unique and sincere contribution to gerontology in Canada: Andrew Martin, President, for his continuing support of the Series; Craig Laudrum, Academic Acquisitions Manager, for his enthusiastic commitment to the promotion and expansion of the Series; and Linda Kee, Assistant Vice-President, Editorial, for her co-ordination of the editorial services. For each of you, we hope the knowledge provided in the Series will have personal value — but not until well into the next century!

Barry McPherson
Series Editor

FOREWORD

While most Canadians live and age in an urban or suburban environment, about 25 percent of our elderly population have lived, and continue to live in rural communities. Contrary to conventional wisdom, less than three percent of elderly Canadians actually live on a farm. Moreover, at least 25 to 30 percent of the residents of many rural villages, towns and communities are over 65 years of age, primarily because of two migration patterns — the outmigration of young people, and/or the in-migration from urban areas of older retirees. Many of these rural residents are elderly widows.

Compared to those who live in an urban community, we know very little about the rural elderly or about aging in a rural community. Yet, it is essential that we study and understand aging in a rural setting because of the unique characteristics, experiences, and lifestyles of life-long rural residents, and because of the unique social structure and demographic profile of this segment of the population. Moreover, while there may be some degree of homogeneity in terms of ethnicity, socioeconomic status, and beliefs and values within a given rural area, there is considerable heterogeneity among the rural communities of Canada. To illustrate, the definition of rural can be applied to a remote fishing outport in Newfoundland, to a farming community in Quebec or Saskatchewan, and to an emerging "retirement" community in the Okanagan valley of British Columbia or in the Niagara peninsula of Ontario. Each of these communities constitutes a rural setting with a different history and economic base, varying distances from metropolitan communities and a different climate. Moreover, the elderly residents of these different rural communities exhibit unique beliefs, values, traditions, occupational and leisure experiences, and incomes.

This diversity, both among rural communities, and when compared to urban settings, needs to be more fully understood and appreciated by students, policy makers and practitioners working with and for the elderly. Some of these unique rural characteristics and challenges include: a belief and value system that stresses both independence and the helping of others; a low population density; a depressed economic base in some localities; the out-migration of children to urban areas; a tendency of farm dwellers to retire at a later age; limited, if any, public transportation; fewer, and less varied, social support and health care services; lower past and current levels of income; a lower level of formal education; lower quality housing; and, less variety in housing options for the later years.

This monograph, written by an author who has lived in and who has friends in a rural community, reviews the limited, but growing body of literature on rural aging. Throughout, understanding of the social reality of rural aging is enhanced by vignettes which present two contrasting experiences — one, of a retired couple who migrated from Vancouver to a rural community in the interior of British Columbia; the other, of a lifelong elderly resident of the same rural community. Throughout the monograph there is a focus on gender differences, on regional differences and on the way native versus non-native elderly Canadians age in a rural environment.

Chapter One provides a historical, cultural and demographic overview of rural traditions from the late 1800s to the 1990s, and presents a thorough and insightful discussion of rurality as a concept. How the concept is defined and operationalized can influence both the questions which are posed by researchers, and the types of programs and policies which are designed for rural residents. Professor Keating, in her analysis of the meaning of "rural", explores three possible thematic determinants: the major occupations of residents; the population density and distance from a metropolitan area; and, the rural ideology as expressed by the belief systems and value orientations of rural residents. The next four chapters focus on topics of particular concern to the rural elderly.

In Chapter Two, lifestyle issues pertaining to work, retirement and leisure are reviewed. First, the labour force participation rates of older rural workers are described, along with some of the unique barriers to participation in the labour force experienced by rural residents. This chapter also includes an interesting discussion of why older rural residents continue to work. Next, the author discusses retirement as an event and as a process within the rural context, and how rural residents adjust to retirement. In a unique contribution to the literature on leisure and aging, Professor Keating describes the heterogeneity of leisure activities, the process whereby leisure activities are adopted, and some possible intervention strategies to change the activity and fitness patterns of rural residents.

A commonly expressed element of the rural ideology is the belief in, and practice of, living independently. Chapter Three presents a definition of independent living held by the rural elderly. This definition includes three components: control over the near environment; integration into the community; and, access to services. Faced with the reality of an older housing stock and fewer housing options, the rural elderly are concerned about losing independence because of the inadequacy of their housing. They are also concerned about the availability of, and access to, needed services so that they can remain integrated in the community. Professor Keating stresses that developing creative solutions for the provision of transportation may not be the most appropriate program or policy to facilitate or ensure the independence of elderly rural residents.

Conventional wisdom has portrayed the rural elderly as having an extended family which provides assistance and care when needed, thereby reducing or eliminating the need for other informal or formal support services. In Chapter Four, these assumptions are carefully addressed through a review of the household structure, the availability of a family network, and the sources, type and amount of family support that is provided to rural residents. Based on this review of existing patterns in different rural settings, the implications for future policies and programs are discussed in the context of an informal system that may be required to provide more support than that found in urban areas.

In Chapter Five, the assumption that the health status of rural elders is lower than that of urban elders is examined. Specifically, Professor Keating reviews the literature on the urban and rural elderly to compare the health beliefs, the physical and mental health status, the perceived health service needs, the utilization rates, and the perceived adequacy of the available or known health services. The chapter concludes with a discussion as to how health promotion programs and practices can be developed and adopted, by both rural practitioners who work with the elderly and by rural seniors.

In the concluding chapter, directions for rural research, policy and practice are proposed. First, however, the author re-examines the definition of rural aging, and concludes that the occupational component should be discarded, and that more emphasis should be placed on the population density and rural ideology components. Furthermore, given the diversity in rural settings, the history of a rural community must also be incorporated into our definition of what constitutes a rural setting. Thus, the author argues that demographic, historical and ideology components should be utilized and stressed in future research pertaining to rural aging. This chapter also introduces important suggestions for determining service needs and for planning service delivery in a rural setting, and concludes by proposing five steps for developing social policies for a rural population.

In summary, this monograph provides a state-of-the-art review and analysis of our limited knowledge about a unique but understudied segment of Canada's older population. While some rural elderly may have a disadvantaged status compared to their urban counterparts, most do not. However, if we are to enhance the quality of life of older rural residents, we need to more fully understand and appreciate the size and diversity of the elderly rural population. Consequently, practitioners and policy-makers with responsibilities in rural settings must become more sensitive to the unique rural ideology, history, and demography of a community or region. With this knowledge and experience they should be in a position to ensure that inappropriate, urban-based policies, programs and practices are not imposed on rural residents. Similarly, students and scholars of rural life must devote greater attention to posing and answering questions about aging in diverse rural environments where the elderly may be lifelong residents or recent in-migrants, where the economic base may be one of poverty or affluence, or where the community may be geographically remote from, or adjacent to, urban areas.

Barry D. McPherson, Ph.D.
Series Editor

Wilfrid Laurier University
Waterloo, Ontario

June, 1991

PREFACE

In many parts of Canada there has been a long sweep of time from the rural beginnings when farmers and trappers settled here, to the urban reality in which many of us now live. Yet we continue to be a country in which our vast natural resources are part of our national pride as well as our economic underpinnings. The 1990s promise to be a decade in which rural Canada will be a focus of attention; from those concerned about the fragile nature of the environment: from those who seek recreational opportunities away from urban centres; from those who choose to live in rural areas once they have retired from their urban jobs.

Perhaps because many Canadians are removed from their rural roots, stereotypes persist about rural life and about growing old in rural Canada. Often these beliefs are in sharp contrast to each other. While we look with nostalgia at the close knit rural family that cared for its elderly members and lived in health and harmony, we perceive a harsh reality in which rural seniors suffer from isolation, lack of health and social services, and a lifetime of harsh physical work.

The purpose of this book is to address some of these assumptions about the lives of rural elders. The increasing popularity of small towns as retirement centres and the departure of young people from rural areas means that many parts of rural Canada have high proportions of seniors. The early part of the book traces some of these changes from our agricultural beginnings and from the development of rural beliefs. Descriptions of the lives of contemporary rural seniors form the major portion of the book. Their patterns of work and retirement, health, and family interaction are discussed, with emphasis on the great variety of experiences of rural dwellers. Throughout the book, vignettes of two urban retirees and a lifelong rural resident are used to illustrate some of the issues of concern to older Canadians. The final chapter points the way to needed research, policy development and service delivery.

This book is intended for rural researchers and practitioners and for students of rural life. It brings together a wide range of information as a resource to those who are developing rural policy and services to rural seniors. May it provide a small measure of assistance in our attempts to ensure that rural aging is more a rural idyll than a precarious existence.

ACKNOWLEDGEMENTS

There are two parts of a book that, for an author, mark its beginning and end. The first is the outline, written with excitement and anticipation. The final is the acknowledgements, written with gratitude. The months in between represent a process of filling an office with hundreds of documents, reading and organizing information, writing and revising, and managing technical and substantive reviews. All is now complete but for the emptying of the office.

From the beginning to the end I have been fortunate to have a group of people who provided technical help, library skills, theoretical challenges, personal insights and caring. Barry McPherson, the series editor, accepted my proposal to write about rural aging. Now that the project is completed, I am glad he did. He read drafts of the manuscript, provided feedback and kept in touch through the wonders of electronic mail while I completed the book on study leave in New Zealand. Butterworths staff members Gloria Vitale, Linda Kee, Edward O'Connor and Agatha Cinader provided excellent technical expertise and feedback, all at a distance. It is a strange process working closely with people you have never met.

I was fortunate to have working with me three graduate students with excellent library skills, energy and commitment to a sometimes tedious task of searching out information. My thanks to Judy Johnson Moodie, Cheryl Raiwet and Priscilla Koop. The reviews of three people with different backgrounds and expertise in rural aging are also greatly appreciated. Dr. Colleen Johnson from the University of California, San Francisco; Dr. Ruth Gasson from Wye College, Kent and Dr. Anne Martin Matthews from the University of Guelph, Ontario made detailed comments on the manuscript and helped me stand back from my work and see how it could be strengthened.

Long chats with my friends in Summerland, British Columbia helped me develop a more informed perspective on aging in one rural part of Canada. Special thanks to Marjorie Croil and Frank and Betty Rose for helping to keep me on track. And I am especially grateful to my best supporter and critic, my husband, Norm Looney. He reorganized his sabbatical so that I could take mine at the right time in the right place, managed my being distracted by chapters that just wouldn't come together and helped carry computers and mountains of paper half way round the world.

CONTENTS

TABLES

FIGURES

PUBLICATIONS ACKNOWLEDGEMENTS

The authors and publishers of the following articles and books have been most generous in giving permission for the reproduction in this text of work already in print. References appear where possible in the text. It is convenient for us to list below, for the assistance of the reader, the publishers and authors for whose courtesy we are most grateful. The following list is organized by author in alphabetical order.

Gower Publishing Co.	J. Brandenburg et al., "A Conceptual Model of How People Adopt Recreation Activities." (1982) Leisure Studies 1:263-276 at p. 269, Figure 1.
Alberta Health	Committee on Long Term Care for Senior Citizens, *A New Vision for Long Term Care: Meeting the Need* at p. 9. Published with permission.
American Geriatrics Society	T. Costello, et al., "Perceptions of Urban versus Rural Hospital Patients about Return to their Communities" (1977). Journal of the American Geriatrics Society 25:552-555 at p. 554, Table 1. Reprinted with permission from the American Geriatrics Society.
Supply and Services, Canada	Health and Welfare Canada and Health Services and Promotions Branch, *Active Health Report on Seniors* (1989), p. 7. Reproduced with permission of the Minister of Supply and Services Canada, 1991.
Canada Mortgage And Housing Corporation	G. Hodge, *Shelter and Services for the Small Town Elderly: The Role of Assisted Housing* (1984).
Supply and Services, Canada	National Advisory Council on Aging, *Moving Ahead with Aging in Canada* (1983). Reproduced with the permission of the Minister of Supply and Services Canada, 1991.
Northern Alberta Development Council, Peace River, Alberta	Regional Steering Committee for Geriatric Services in the North Peace River Region, *A New Beginning: A Review of the Needs of Seniors in the Peace River Health Unit* (1986).

Supply and Ser-   Statistics Canada, *Population Labour Force — Occupation by*
vices, Canada   *Demographic and Educational Characteristics, 1981* Catalogue 92-
                  917 (1984), data from Table 2. Reproduced with permission of
                  the Minister of Supply and Services Canada, 1991.

Supply and Ser-   Statistics Canada, *Occupied Private Dwellings, 1981 Census*
vices, Canada   Catalogue #93-932, (1984), Table 7. Reproduced with the per-
                  mission of the Minister of Supply and Services Canada, 1991.

Supply and Ser-   Statistics Canada, *Census Canada 1986 Reference Dictionary,*
vices, Canada   Catalogue #99-101E (1987), pp. 53, 127. Reproduced with the
                  permission of the Minister of Supply and Services Canada,
                  1991.

Supply and Ser-   Statistics Canada, *Profiles — Urban and Rural Areas, Canada,*
vices, Canada   *Provinces and Territories Part 1, 1986.* Catalogue #94-129
                  (1988),Table. Reproduced with the permission of the Minister
                  of Supply and Services Canada, 1991.

Newfoundland,   J.B. Vivian, *Home Support Services Survey Project* Vol. 2 (1982).
Department of
Social Services

CHAPTER 1

RURAL ROOTS

INTRODUCTION

Now in its second century since confederation, Canada is still close to its rural beginnings. In some areas of the country there are elderly people who, as youths, cleared their land with horse and plough and now live in the relative comfort that has come with technological change. In other areas are those who continue to harvest natural resources: fish, lumber, minerals. Agriculture still generates more than half of the economic activity of some of the prairie provinces (Alberta Agriculture, 1988), although it is no longer central to the Canadian economy as a whole.

The historic predominance of agriculture in Canada has shaped our definitions of "rural" and influenced the lives of contemporary rural seniors. Like other countries in which farming has been central, Canada still uses economic activity in agriculture as the basis for defining what is rural. In Canada, "rural" includes farm and non-farm. In contrast, countries with high population densities like Japan, use "rural" as the residual category after taking into account urban economic activity in manufacturing and trade (United Nations, 1986). Census definitions determine the proportion of seniors who are officially counted as rural.

The emergence of "urban" as a census category is important because, historically, Canada was primarily agriculture-based. Urban Canada stretches along our southern border. The uneven population distribution means that while many rural seniors may live close to a metropolitan centre, some are still geographically isolated. The heterogeneous living situations of rural seniors are a recent development in Canadian history.

Out of their experiences, pioneer farmers are believed to have developed a set of values that is generally assumed to still be held by rural Canadians. The interconnection of work and family life, the need to control the natural environment, and geographic isolation are thought to have fostered a strong "rural ideology" which emphasized independence and family ties. It is possible that seniors still espouse this "rural ideology" even if they have long since moved away from the farm.

Occupation, population density and ideological facets of rurality form the basis for the definition of "rural" discussed later in this chapter. Each of these aspects of rural life raises different questions about the nature of being

1

old in rural Canada. Do seniors with farm backgrounds experience aging differently than those who have no history in agriculture? Does the rural milieu affect elders positively because of the supportiveness and stability of rural communities, or negatively because of the distances from health and social services and because of the lack of public transportation? To what extent have rural elders a set of beliefs about work, leisure, family and independence that are different from those held by urban elders? How much does rurality affect aging and how much does aging influence the nature of rural communities?

The purpose of this chapter is to provide a historical overview of rural traditions in Canada and of the aging of the rural population over the last century. A brief look at settlement patterns, early rural beliefs and the development of definitions of rural life provide the backdrop for the issues that are discussed in detail in subsequent chapters. The remainder of the book is devoted to issues affecting rural Canadian seniors today.

CANADA'S RURAL TRADITIONS: A DEMOGRAPHIC OVERVIEW

In 1867 the area that is now Canada had a population of 3.5 million people, 2.5 million of whom lived in Ontario and Quebec (Leacy, 1983). The settlement of the Prairies had just begun, in order to prevent American expansion north of the forty-ninth parallel and to link central and eastern Canada with British Columbia (Tyler, 1968). Manitoba became the seventh province in 1870, with Saskatchewan and Alberta following 35 years later in 1905.

Although the Prairies have been described by European historians as previously unsettled, native peoples had lived in the area for approximately 12,000 years (Wilson, 1986). The introduction of trade in guns, horses and furs with the arrival of the Europeans brought the two groups into an economic partnership, with each group having some control of trade and the way of life on which it was based (Fisher, 1986). However, by the twentieth century the European-Canadians had gained control. "Since the 1920s they (the Indians) have been forcefully excluded from the economic life of western Canada" (Fisher, 1986: 373). This exclusion has had far-reaching consequences for subsequent generations of native peoples in Canada. The forced integration of native peoples into the larger society accompanied racial barriers to upward socio-economic mobility (Ponting, 1986). Although predominantly a rural people, high rates of infant mortality and violent death have meant that few of Canada's indigenous people reached old age and today the native rural elderly make up a small percentage of the rural elderly in Canada. The life expectancy of Indian men and women is still about ten years less than it is for the rest of the population (Rowe and Norris, 1985).

Immigration into the prairies by non-natives was encouraged by the Homestead Act of 1886 which made ownership of land possible for people with little capital. "The lure of land ownership, with its traditional correlates of freedom, security and status, brought settlers from agricultural and non-agricultural backgrounds, from a variety of ethnic groups, religious denominations, and cultural traditions" (Tyler, 1968: 248). Settlers came because of the land, as they had done generations earlier in other parts of the country.

Rural Occupations

The 1890-91 census shows Canada to be a society characterized by "the extraction from nature of the means of livelihood" (Whyte, 1968: 5). The majority of Canadian men were involved in agriculture, fishing or mining. The percentage of men involved in these primary industries varied somewhat across the country with a high of 70 percent in Prince Edward Island and a low of 35 percent in British Columbia. Unlike Prince Edward Island, British Columbia had only a small amount of land suitable for farming. However, agriculture, fishing and mining were the largest occupational categories in both provinces. Many workers in other occupational sectors were involved in activities that were supportive to primary industries. Hunters, trappers, scouts and guides were included in the category of domestic and personal service. Those employed in manufacturing and mechanical industries included blacksmiths, agricultural implement makers, fish curers and packers, harness and saddle makers, meat packers, curers and picklers, and ship and boat builders. Veterinary surgeons were included under the category of professionals. Those working in trade and transportation included boarding and livery stablekeepers, pilots and sailors.

This was not a society of older people. The retired were placed in the category of non-productive, along with Indian chiefs, members of religious orders, paupers, inmates in asylums and students!

According to the 1890-91 census tabulations, few Canadian women were involved in the primary industries of agriculture, fishing and mining. The census records that an average of 6 percent of women across Canada were employed in these primary industries, with the largest percentage in Nova Scotia (11 percent) and the smallest in New Brunswick (1 percent) (Bureau of Statistics, 1893). Yet, there are early reports of farm women's heavy farm and domestic work loads that belie these statistics. In fact, at the turn of the century, the job of running a farm household was shared equally by men and women who worked an average of eleven hours a day (Vanek, 1980). Women's tasks included work in the garden, care of poultry, milking, pruning fruit trees, picking and packing fruit, pumping water, carrying wood, fieldwork and chores (Vanek, 1980; Vester, 1982; Wilkening, 1981). The majority of women who were counted as having occupations were in domestic and personal service, with most employed as servants and dress-makers.

Table 1.1 gives information on the number of men and women involved in various primary occupations in 1891. Farming and related occupations involved the largest proportion of men and women in all of the provinces. Farmers' sons were an occupational category, indicating the importance placed on generational transfer of farm operations. However, in the maritime provinces on both coasts, a substantial number of people were also involved in fishing. For the next 100 years there continued to be relatively few people involved in farming in British Columbia because of the small amount of arable land in the province.

Historically the small number of women recorded as employed in primary occupations is partly due to the undercounting of women in "male" occupations; for instance there has never been a census category of farmers' daughters to parallel that of farmers' sons. Even so, there have historically been more men than women in rural Canada. In 1921 there were 129 rural men aged 55 to 69 and 113 men over age 70 for each 100 women of the same age (Whyte, 1968). Highest ratios of men to women for the 70+ group are found in the west, which is the most recently settled part of the country. Farm populations have always had the highest ratios of males to females of any rural group. In 1981, the sex ratio for the Canadian farm population over age 70 was 117 males for every 100 females as compared to 105 for the non-farm population (Statistics Canada, 1982). Unlike contemporary urban Canada with its preponderance of elderly women, rural Canada has always had more older men.

The occupations of Canadians in the mid-to-late-nineteenth century reflect what Whyte (1968) argues is a fundamental difference between urban and rural ways of life. The wheat farmer of the prairies and the farmer-fisherman-lumberman of Quebec or the Maritimes were oriented to predominantly natural forces. Their goals were to triumph over the natural environment. "In a completely rural society, the non-social environment is the major independent variable, the social environment being primarily an effect rather than a cause" (Whyte, 1968:5). Farming was the economic focus of rural life for men and women of all ages.

The Shift from Rural to Urban

By the end of the nineteenth century urban Canada was beginning to develop. The census of 1871 recorded .75 million urban residents and three million rural residents (Leacy, 1983). "Urban" was broadly defined to include all incorporated cities, towns and villages, regardless of size (Statistics Canada, 1987a). By 1921, the majority of Canadians were classified as urban, although there were great regional differences. In the Atlantic

TABLE 1.1

PRIMARY OCCUPATIONS OF 1891 (AGRICULTURE, FISHING, AND MINING)

MALES & FEMALES OVER 15 YEARS

	BC		MAN		NB		NS		ONT		PEI		QUE	
	M	F	M	F	M	F	M	F	M	F	M	F	M	F
Apiarists	3	—	4	—	7	2	9	29	97	14	—	1	6	2
Dairymen & Women	45	1	38	2	46	—	80	8	539	28	4	—	98	6
Farm Labourers	1759	9	4981	21	5046	13	7491	79	39,805	146	1546	5	14,201	61
Farmers	4472	75	20,322	252	28,333	904	32,611	1948	174,321	5245	12,037	419	117,407	2645
Farmer's Sons	732	—	5353	—	12,259	—	13,593	—	86,251	—	5903	—	53,509	—
Fishermen	3743	54	79	—	2884	13	14,136	95	1408	6	904	3	3412	21
Garden & Nursery Labourers	227	—	71	—	53	—	155	2	1745	11	20	—	501	20
Gardeners, Florists & Nurserymen	179	3	59	1	75	—	49	5	2165	39	13	—	455	28
Lumbermen & Raftsmen	1119	—	85	—	1236	—	1509	—	4030	—	95	—	4174	—
Miners	4566	—	9	—	96	—	5419	—	1029	—	18	—	1514	—
Officials of Mines & Quarries	42	—	—	—	12	—	93	—	48	—	—	—	43	—
Quarrymen	55	—	50	—	230	—	85	—	572	—	6	—	525	—
Stockherders & Drovers	85	—	56	—	6	—	21	—	165	—	1	—	158	—
Stock Raisers	110	2	103	—	2	—	2	—	27	—	—	—	8	1
Wood Choppers	285	—	9	—	5	—	1	—	132	—	—	—	25	—
Other Agricultural Pursuits	2	—	1	—	2	—	2	—	97	21	—	—	14	—

SOURCE: Bureau of Statistics (1893) *Occupations Census of Canada 1890-91*, Vol. 2, Table XII, Ottawa: E. Dawson

region, until 1962, the majority of residents were counted as rural. In contrast, Ontario was primarily rural only until 1901; Quebec until 1911. In British Columbia, the majority of residents were classified as rural until 1921. Those among todays seniors, who grew up in Atlantic Canada or the Prairies are likely to have rural backgrounds while those who were raised in central Canada or British Columbia are likely to have urban backgrounds. Today, seniors who grew up in Canada do not all have rural roots.

Despite its agricultural heritage, much of the history of Canada has been typified by reductions in the number of people involved in agriculture. Before 1900, agriculture was the major occupation in central Canada and the Prairies; more recently, there has been a shift away from agriculture. The farm population in Canada has been declining for the past 50 years (Leacy, 1983), most dramatically since the Second World War (Whyte, 1968). There are regional differences in this decline, with peaks in farm populations occurring later in the west. For example, while the largest farm populations in Prince Edward Island, Nova Scotia and New Brunswick were reached in 1931, in British Columbia the peak was reached in 1951.

The 1960s and 1970s brought dramatic changes to rural life across Canada. Continued technological improvement in primary industries such as farming, combined with labour shortages in cities, meant that over one million people left farming areas (Hodge and Collins, 1987). Since the majority of these migrants were young, their departure contributed to an increase in the average age of the farm population. Thus, although the absolute numbers of people in farming declined, the proportion of older farmers increased. In fact, the 1986 census is the first in decades in which the number of older operators increased in absolute terms. In 1986, 34 percent of census farm operators were over age 55, the highest proportion since the Second World War (Statistics Canada, 1987b).

At the same time that people were leaving farming, urban people began to move out of the cities into open countryside and small towns. The net result was that rural Canada in 1981 was larger by 1.7 million people than it had been 20 years earlier. The occupations and backgrounds of its residents were also more diverse. Both the movement of people out of farming and the in-migration to rural areas has dramatically changed the rural countryside and the milieu in which rural residents grow old (Hodge and Collins, 1987).

Regional Differences

The lives of rural Canadians in the last century were not homogeneous across the country. One reason for the differences lies in the timing of settlement and the nature of settlement patterns across the country. Two examples serve to illustrate this point.

When Saskatchewan became a province in 1905, the railway had recently been constructed and an open immigration policy brought thousands of new people to the province. Few of these people were seniors. The great majority were young, single men, who established farms in the province (Senior Citizens Provincial Council, 1983). Twenty-five years later, the Depression saw the population decline, as young people left the dust bowl to look for work. Between 1931 and 1941 the farm population decreased by almost 50,000 (Leacy, 1983). During these difficult times, farms were able to support fewer people, a situation conducive to neither the development of multigeneration farms nor to the persistence of large extended families living in close proximity. Out-migration continued through the 1950s as increasing mechanization of agriculture reduced the need for large numbers of people to work the farm. By 1961, the agricultural labour force in the prairies was only 66 percent of what it had been in 1941 (Whyte, 1968).

The result of these early migration and settlement patterns and the later out-migration of young people has meant that Saskatchewan now has a higher proportion of seniors (13 percent) than does any other province in Canada (Statistics Canada, 1987b). The early waves of immigrants consisted predominantly of men and there is still a relatively high ratio of elderly men to women in this province.

In contrast, in 1905 Quebec had been a province for two generations and had had permanent settlements for over 150 years. Within francophone Quebec, the three generation rural family already had a long tradition. Rural Quebec has always had the largest average size of any rural families in the country (Whyte, 1968). The Roman Catholic church has traditionally sanctioned large families because those families strengthened the role of the church in rural parishes. Approximately half of the two million residents in Quebec were rural (Whyte, 1968), with about 20 percent of rural residents involved in farming. Thus, while Saskatchewan was an agricultural province inhabited by first generation immigrants, Quebec was more established, had a broader work base of rural residents and had a stronger family tradition (Quebec Ministry of Social Services, 1985).

It was not until the Quiet Revolution of the 1960s that life for rural Quebec families and, hence, for rural elders began to change. Some have argued that the shift from a traditional to a post-industrial society was accompanied by a shift in values toward a nuclear family household and toward individuality and personal achievement (Quebec Ministry of Social Services, 1985). Others suggest that the French Canadian rural family is more impervious to the inroads of change because kinship systems are part of strongly held cultural values based in rural and religious traditions (Whyte, 1968).

These descriptions of settlement patterns in two different parts of the country show the roots of diversity in rural Canada. Different traditions in patterns of work, family structure, settlement, migration and religious values all have the potential to influence the lives of seniors in different regions.

Immigration

One aspect of the heterogeneity of rural life in Canada has been the immigration of different ethnic groups. These groups were often recruited and settled separately, resulting in "German" or "English" or "Ukranian" communities. Ethnicity has a powerful impact on rural communities, influencing the type of farming done in an area, the social structure of communities, the physical layout of towns and the community values (Flynn, 1987).

In a review of Canada's ethnic elders, Bond (1986) traced some of the changes in immigration of different ethnic groups. Between 1871 and 1971 there has been an decrease in the number of immigrants born in the United Kingdom and the United States; an increase of those born in Italy, Greece, Portugal, and the Netherlands; and fluctuating patterns of immigration from Germany, Austria, Poland and Russia. Many rural areas of Canada settled by groups of immigrants still reflect a strong ethnic bias. For example, one group of farmers came from the Netherlands to northern Alberta in 1911. They developed a farming community around a village called Neerlandia. Today, second, third and fourth generation farmers still farm in the much expanded community. Ninety-six percent of the residents are of Dutch background and "reformed" religion (Neerlandia Historical Society, 1985).

Future cohorts of rural elders may have quite different ethnic backgrounds. Of the 142,000 immigrants entering Canada in 1980, 50 percent arrived from Asia, 29 percent from Europe, and 12 percent from the United States and West Indies. Only 1 percent of those immigrants were over the age of 65 (Bond, 1986). Thus, in the near future we will presumably have few elders who are adapting to a new country. However, depending upon where they settle, the needs, interests and expectations of rural elders in upcoming generations may be quite different than they are today. Since most immigrants come to Ontario, British Columbia, Quebec and Alberta (Statistics Canada, 1990), the nature of aging in those provinces may become quite different than in those provinces with little immigration. As well, increased interest on the part of native peoples in the restoration of their lands and heritage and an increase in the size of the native population (Ponting, 1986) will add to the mosaic of rural elders.

In summary, although Canada has been populated for more than 12,000 years, the heritage of most of Canada's rural elders comes from more recent immigrants who acquired land and produced food for personal consumption and for trade. Although the number of farmers has declined over the last 100 years, a large proportion of Canada's elders still have close connections to their farm backgrounds and beliefs. Regional differences in settlement patterns, organization of these agricultural communities and religious life mean, however, that the lives of elders in different parts of the country vary greatly.

Contemporary Rural Seniors

Table 1.2 shows the percentages of rural farm and non-farm seniors living in all provinces and territories of Canada. Canada now has many more urban than rural seniors, although proportions are not evenly distributed across the country. The Maritime provinces still have large rural populations and Prince Edward Island has more rural than urban seniors. In contrast, British Columbia continues to be an urban province with four times as many urban as rural seniors.

Rural seniors are underrepresented among farmers. Only 6.1 percent of rural farm residents are seniors, compared to 9.7 percent who live in non-farm areas. Even though they are self-employed, most farmers do retire and move off the farm.

Northern Canada (the Yukon and Northwest Terrorities) has a very small percentage of seniors. Lower life expectancy of native seniors and a large population of young people working in resource industries contribute to this bias in both rural and urban parts of the north.

The historical demographic pictures of settlement in rural Canada and of the demography of contemporary rural seniors illustrate one aspect of the lives of seniors in various parts of the country. However, population statistics are only one way of understanding the lives of rural seniors or even of determining who is rural. As seen in the following discussion on definitions of the term "rural", value orientations and occupations are other facets which contribute to the complexity of rural life.

A DEFINITION OF RURAL

The definition of the term "rural" has evolved and changed as much as has rural life itself. Some have argued that rural life is now so diverse that it is impossible to define. "There is now, surely, a general awareness that what constitutes "rural" is wholly a matter of convenience and that arid and abstract definitional exercises are of little utility" (Newby, 1986: 209). Newby's statement is probably a reaction to one of the major frustrations in the study of rural life. Despite a good deal of discussion in the literature, there is still no consensus on the definition of rural. Nonetheless, one must take exception to Newby's rejection of the task. As will become evident in this book, the way in which one defines rural has a profound effect on the questions posed by researchers and the programs and policies developed for rural areas. The very complexity of the concept makes its definition

TABLE 1.2

RURAL SENIORS: CANADA, PROVINCES AND TERRITORIES

		Total	Total Urban	Total Rural	Rural Non-Farm	Rural Farm
CANADA	TOTAL	25,309,330	19,352,085	5,957,245	5,066,760	890,490
	65+	2,456,695	1,912,605	544,090	489,615	54,475
	% 65+	9.7	9.9	9.1	9.7	6.1
NEWFOUNDLAND	TOTAL	568,345	334,730	233,615	231,930	1,685
	65+	46,445	26,760	19,680	19,575	105
	% 65+	8.2	8.0	8.4	8.4	6.2
PRINCE EDWARD ISLAND	TOTAL	126,650	48,290	78,355	68,085	10,275
	65+	14,560	6,165	8,395	7,495	900
	% 65+	11.5	12.8	10.7	11.0	8.8
NOVA SCOTIA	TOTAL	873,175	471,130	402,045	387,875	14,175
	65+	96,775	52,090	44,685	43,460	1,220
	% 65+	11.1	11.1	11.1	11.2	8.6
NEW BRUNSWICK	TOTAL	709,445	350,300	359,135	347,025	12,110
	65+	72,575	39,530	33,045	32,095	945
	% 65+	10.2	11.3	9.2	9.3	7.8
QUEBEC	TOTAL	6,532,460	5,088,995	1,443,465	1,300,085	143,380
	65+	579,025	465,185	113,840	107,415	6,425
	% 65+	8.9	9.1	7.9	8.3	4.5
ONTARIO	TOTAL	9,101,695	7,469,420	1,632,275	1,399,485	232,790
	65+	911,400	757,935	153,465	136,780	16,685
	% 65+	10.0	10.2	9.4	9.8	7.2

TABLE 1.2, CONT'D

RURAL SENIORS: CANADA, PROVINCES AND TERRITORIES

		Total	Total Urban	Total Rural	Rural Non-Farm	Rural Farm
MANITOBA	TOTAL	1,063,015	766,855	296,160	211,475	84,690
	65+	122,385	90,780	31,605	26,585	5,025
	% 65+	11.5	11.8	10.7	12.6	5.9
SASKATCHEWAN	TOTAL	1,009,615	620,200	389,420	227,920	161,495
	65+	117,880	71,975	45,905	35,845	10,065
	% 65+	11.7	11.6	11.8	15.7	6.2
ALBERTA	TOTAL	2,365,825	1,877,755	488,065	309,950	178,115
	65+	170,845	133,270	37,580	27,870	9,705
	% 65+	7.2	7.1	7.7	9.0	5.5
B.C.	TOTAL	2,883,370	2,285,005	598,360	546,590	51,775
	65+	322,690	268,120	54,570	51,175	3,395
	% 65+	11.2	11.7	9.1	9.4	6.6
YUKON	TOTAL	23,505	15,195	8,305	8,305	—
	65+	790	430	360	360	—
	% 65+	3.4	2.8	4.3	4.3	—
N.W.T.	TOTAL	52,235	24,210	28,025	28,025	—
	65+	1,325	385	940	945	—
	% 65+	2.5	1.6	3.4	3.4	—

SOURCE: Statistics Canada (1988d). *Profiles — Urban and Rural Areas, Canada, Provinces and Territories Part 1, 1986*. Catalogue #94-129, Table. Ottawa: Minister of Supply and Services Canada.

critical to the understanding of the variety of experiences of the elderly in rural Canada.

Two examples will be used throughout the book to illustrate the difficulties of defining both "rural" and "elderly".

Kaslo, B.C. is located on Kootenay Lake in the interior of British Columbia, 600 km east of Vancouver. It was first settled in 1892 during a silver mining boom. In its early history, Kaslo was destroyed by a flood on the Kootenay river but it was subsequently rebuilt. After the First World War mining declined but fruit farming and logging developed. Kaslo now has a population of 1,100 people who are involved in logging and sawmilling as well as in the tourist trade (The Canadian Encyclopaedia, 1985: 934). Kaslo has a population of 1100.

Ruth Wilson was born and raised in Vancouver. For 30 years she worked for the province of British Columbia. The last ten years before she retired at age 62, she was an Assistant Deputy Minister. She and her husband, Al, retired at the same time. Al had been a senior executive with a large insurance company. He had grown up in a small town in Ontario and was looking forward to retiring to the countryside. Three years ago they moved to the village of Kaslo.

Murray Nelson was a miner's son, born about 10 km from Kaslo. Murray's family eked out a living by mining and subsistence farming. Now 78, Murray still farms the family homestead. For 50 years he has also been the bartender in the Kaslo hotel.

While the Wilsons and Murray Nelson are both "elderly" and both live in the same area, their experiences and ways of living may be expected to be quite different. In order to make sense of these differences and similarities we must analyze the components of rurality.

Although there are many definitions of rural, the most common include one or more of three elements: occupation; population density; and rural ideology.

In the next section of this chapter, these three components of rural life will be discussed and the question of whether it is appropriate to use urban markers of old age in a rural setting will be considered.

Occupation

Until 1961, the Canadian census had no occupational designation of rural. Some would argue that none was required because the general term "rural" referred to a population that derived the majority of its livelihood from agricultural production or related industries such as mining and fishing

(Atchley and Byerts, 1975; Miller and Luloff, 1981). Until recently, in Canada "rural" was synonymous with "agricultural".

Since 1961, the census category of rural has been divided into farm and non-farm subcategories. This change has resulted from an acknowledgement that the economic base of rural parts of the country is now broader than agriculture (Watkins and Watkins, 1984). Under this census designation, the occupational category of farm is defined as "all persons living in rural areas who are members of the households of farm operators living on their farms for any length of time during the 12 month period prior to the census" (Statistics Canada, 1987a). A census farm is "any agricultural holding with sales of agricultural products of $250 or more during the 12 month period prior to the census" (Statistics Canada, 1987a). Rural non-farm became a residual category referring to "all persons living in rural areas who are not members of the households of farm operators living on their farms for any length of time during the 12 month period prior to the census" (Statistics Canada, 1987a). Rural now includes one group defined by their occupation and another which is not.

Some have lamented the shift away from seeing farming as the only "genuinely rural" endeavour. For them, rural people must, by definition, be involved in the occupation of farming (Maclouf and Lion, 1983). Others see the inclusion of a non-farm category as long overdue since western countries have become urbanized economically, occupationally, socially and culturally (Newby, 1986).

Whether or not those who are farmers are more rural than those who are not, there are several advantages to having two categories of rural. First, it allows us to compare the lives of those who have been farmers with those who have not. Of the people from Kaslo described earlier in this chapter, Murray Nelson would be classified as a farmer because he had sales of over $250 from his farm. This designation is made regardless of the fact that Murray's major source of income has always been from his "town" job. Ruth and Al Wilson have never farmed or drawn income from agriculture. Yet they chose to live in Kaslo because they see it as a rural, agricultural area. But since they live in Kaslo, which is too large to be classified as rural non-farm, they would not be seen as rural.

The farm/non-farm distinction also allows us to track the changes in rural occupational structures from farming to other endeavours. Being a farmer in an area primarily devoted to farming may be quite a different experience than being a farmer in a tourist area.

Finally, it allows us to consider the interrelationships between the occupational structure and the roles and status of rural residents. As a long time resident, Murray Nelson is known by his farm and village jobs. As retired newcomers, previous occupation may be less relevant as a way to place the Wilsons in the community.

Population Density/Distance

Occupation is only one criterion used to define types of rural residents. Additional criteria used to define rurality include population density and distance from metropolitan centres. In Canada, the current census definition of a rural area is one in which the population is less than 1,000 people, with a population density of less than 400 per square km (Statistics Canada, 1987a). In the United States, a rural area is defined more liberally as an area with a population of less than 2,500, thereby making it impossible to make direct comparisons between the two countries. Population definitions of "rural" have also changed over time. In 1900 in the United States, places with populations under 4,000 were considered rural. In 1910 the number was changed to 2,500 (Adams, 1975).

A concept related to population density is distance from large population centres or service centres. In Canada there is no census definition which takes distance into account. Thus, the village of Caledon East, 20 km northwest of Toronto, is treated in the same way as the village of South Indian Lake, 600 km north of Winnipeg. Flynn (1987: 389), says that outside of a narrow population band near the United States border, the typical rural community in Canada is "an isolated outpost dependent upon a single export product." Yet that narrow population band encompasses a large group of people and not all rural communities are geographically isolated. Distance from larger population or service centres is a variable that should be used to define "rural" and it is unfortunate that there is no Canadian census category which takes this variable into account.

In contrast to Canada, the United States has a category "metropolitan-rural" that includes areas which would be considered rural on the basis of their population densities, but which are located within the county boundaries of a metropolitan area. The category of metropolitan-rural addresses the issue of the influence of a large metropolitan centre (Miller and Luloff, 1981).

At the other extreme from metropolitan-rural are areas which are called "remote-rural" because of their distance from large population areas. Canadian seniors are considered by some health service providers to be living in remote areas if services such as acute or extended health care facilities are not locally available (Regional Steering Committee for Geriatric Services in the North Peace River Region (hereinafter called Peace River Health Unit), 1986). The actual distance from a large population or service centre for an area to be considered remote varies from country to country and is tempered by elements of cultural, economic and social remoteness.

Cultural remoteness is typified by specific forms of culture that are being vigorously kept alive. The Mennonite settlements in central Ontario and the Hutterite colonies of southern Alberta represent groups that are remote because of their cultural distinctiveness, although they may not be geographically remote. Economic and social remoteness are defined by Stalwick (1983) as those areas bypassed by economic development and having forms of social life that are rare elsewhere. Northern fishing villages in Newfoundland and some of the native communities of the Northwest Territories are examples. Many remote populations have high proportions of elderly residents, a reflection of their social marginalization (Maclouf and Lion, 1983). Whether seniors in remote rural areas are relatively advantaged or disadvantaged remains to be investigated.

If distance from a large urban centre is used as the determining factor of rurality, then both the Wilsons and Murray Nelson are rural since the area in which they live is 600 km from a major metropolitan area. Yet, following the population density definition of rural, only Murray Nelson is considered rural because he lives outside of Kaslo, in an area of low population density. The Wilsons are not rural since they live in Kaslo which has a population of 1,100. One might question whether the experiences of living within or just outside a small, remote community are significantly different. Martin Matthews (1988a: 144) argues that life in a town of 2,000 is typically more similar to life in a village of 500 than to life in a city of 25,000 inhabitants. "The town, although urban by definition, is often decidedly rural in character." The contrast between a town and a city of over one million must seem even more dramatic to recent arrivals like the Wilsons.

Population density definitions of rural have been problematic, since their variation between and within countries precludes accurate comparisons over time. These types of definitions fail to address the character or the complexity of rural life, as was indicated in the example of the residents from Kaslo. Definitions based on population density are subject to misinterpretation in cases where unincorporated towns are lumped into a rural non-farm category regardless of their population. Significant miscalculations may occur in communities where migrant miners and trappers are not counted because of extended absence from their home communities (Hodge and Collins, 1987). Perhaps the most important problem is the fact that those who are remote because of their cultural distinctiveness are not taken into account in this definition.

Rural Ideology

Early immigrants to rural Canada developed a value orientation influenced by their lives on the harsh northern frontier. Their beliefs about the world influenced their lives and thinking and are still part of what is known today as the "rural ideology". Understanding the value orientations of early rural Canadians provides a beginning in the quest to understanding rural residents, especially rural seniors. Their values inform us about orientations to time, activity and relationships and their assumptions concerning human nature, and the relationship between people and the environment. (Kluckhohn, 1958).

Part of early rural ideology was a belief that people were basically evil but perfectible. This idea was inherited in part from American Puritans who felt that only with constant control and self-discipline could goodness be achieved (Kluckhohn, 1958). Behaviours that illustrate this value are seen in Youman's (1967) description of farm and small town life in the United States at the beginning of this century. He described these farmers as rigid and patriarchal with a belief in a strict fundamentalist religion. Control over self and family was considered important.

A second aspect of value systems is the way in which the relationship between people and nature is understood. Rural dwellers, especially farmers, have traditionally been seen as having a fatalistic orientation toward nature, believing that there is little to be done about such phenomena as storms, drought, etc. These attitudes developed from the impact of the physical environment on early settlers. Many settlers had little or no farming experience and even those who had been farmers were often ill-prepared for the harsh northern climate (Blackburn, 1987). Yet one reason that settlers came to the Canadian frontier was because they had a belief in their abilities to overcome nature. A great emphasis on the ability of technology to overcome natural obstacles in order to do such things as span rivers, clear land or find cures for diseases, is still seen among contemporary rural seniors (Raiwet, 1989).

Rural Canadians have historically been oriented toward the future, and toward an active life. Immigrants came to Canada because of opportunities and lack of constraints offered by a new country. They were, therefore, open to change and tended to reject anything "old fashioned" (Kluckhohn, 1958).

The final element of value orientations is the relationships of people to other people. Historically, in Canada, individual autonomy was both necessary and highly valued since most rural dwellers were self-employed. However, cooperative relationships with neighbours as well as with family members were also fundamental to survival. Settlers used trial and error to develop farming methods and found that the exchange of information about successes and failures was invaluable. The family farm became not only the production unit, but also the unit through which groups of people organized to develop local institutions such as churches and schools. Since most had come from areas where such institutions were well-established, there was high value placed on initiatives to develop these institutions in new communities. Family networks were not just a matter of sentiment but were crucial to survival.

Canadian and American beliefs about the values that made up the rural ideology are similar. Bilby and Benson (1977) describe American rural ideology as being conservative in religion, right-wing in politics, supportive of a strong nuclear family, economically frugal, hard-working and individualistic. The Canadian version is similar with an emphasis on interdependence of family, friends and neighbours, a spirit of self-determination and self-reliance, and a negative attitude toward receiving charity (Mark, 1981).

This summary of the characteristics of rural culture is inevitably limited because it does not acknowledge the variations in rural culture. There may be several rural ideologies which differ according to differences in occupation, ethnicity and distance from metropolitan areas. While farmers may come from a tradition in which economic frugality was necessary, professionals who retire to rural areas may have learned to enjoy relative economic affluence.

There may also be regional differences in rural ideologies. Region is an objective term for a territorially-based unit with distinctive social, cultural and psychological characteristics. Regionalism is the identification of regional differences (Matthews, 1983). It has three elements: identity, identification and commitment. "Identity" is the significance of the region in the individual's personal identity. "Identification" is the degree to which a person identifies with a region. "Commitment" is the level of commitment a person has to a region. Using these three characteristics, a prairie regionalist might be defined as someone whose identity is that of prairie farmer even 20 years after retirement from farming, who when asked where he is from, says 'the Prairies', and who wouldn't move to another area under any circumstances. In contrast, a maritime regionalist might have an identity based on fishing, an identification with the sea and a strong commitment to a region that may never be able to offer more than a modest standard of living.

Even within one geographical area, there may be variations in regionalism. For example, although populations of elders in the eastern and western Northwest Territories share similar ethnic backgrounds and physical environments, their lives are quite different. The Dene people have band councils which organize services, such as homemaking and woodcutting, to the community. The Inuit in the eastern Northwest Territories see relatives, neighbours and friends as responsible for looking after dependent members of the community. For them, there is a certain loss of esteem when support services are utilized (Guemple, 1980).

It seems unlikely that rural seniors hold a single set of beliefs about rural life. Regional, occupational, cultural and population density differences all influence rural ideology. Similarly, there is some indication that beliefs about rural life are developed early and that those with the strongest identification with rural areas grew up in those areas. Urban seniors who move to rural areas at retirement are less satisfied with the move than are those who are returning to their rural roots (Cape, 1984). These urban seniors may cause some disruption to rural areas if they do not have the same values as the original older population (Maclouf and Lion, 1983). A mix of long-term residents and in-migrants could transform the model of aging in the rural environment (Martin Matthews, 1988a) as much as could the shift from farm to non-farm. Thus, it seems imperative that we include rural ideologies in the definition of what is rural.

The difficulty of using "rural ideology" as a criterion to measure "rurality" becomes evident if we refer back to the examples of the Wilsons and Murray Nelson. Al Wilson may have a different view of rural than his wife since he grew up in a small town and she was raised in an urban area. Murray Nelson may hold traditional rural values based on his farming background, or less traditional ones, modified by his 'town' job. Despite a wide range of values, all of these people may consider themselves to be rural.

Being Old in Rural Canada

The three aspects of rural discussed in this chapter provide the basis, in this monograph, for the investigation of aging in rural Canada. Where possible, discussion includes comparisons between farm and non-farm seniors; between those in remote areas and those with easy access to metropolitan centres; and among those with different ethnic or cultural backgrounds. Rural ideologies have not been explored extensively but rural values are evident in such areas as attitudes toward work and health and these attitudes are discussed in subsequent chapters. Comparisons are made with urban dwellers where these comparisons seem relevant. In this monograph the perspective is not held that "rural" is a residual category of "urban" or that the only way we can understand rural issues is to compare them with urban issues. Reliance on a population density continuum is insufficient to capture the heterogeneity of the rural population (Martin Matthews, 1988b).

The analysis of rural aging is timely since rural areas and rural ideologies are experiencing fundamental change. In the past few decades, rural areas of many western countries have been by-passed by planners because of government decisions to focus planning and resource allocation on urban centres. Some would argue that these decisions led to the marginalization of communities that were farthest from the overall plans, both geographically and culturally (Maclouf and Lion, 1983). From this perspective, rural elders are especially vulnerable in a technocratic society; left with traditions of self-reliance, but with few resources to sustain them (Harbert and Wilkinson, 1979).

Although the previous discussion may lead the reader to think that this book is about the plight of the rural elderly, it is important to balance the evidence of the disadvantages of the rural elderly with a discussion of how we determine disparity. Regional disparity (in this case rural-urban disparity) is defined as inequality in the availability of some or all of the normally available resources, services, capital, etc. (Matthews 1983). Deciding that a region is disadvantaged is always a subjective judgement, since there is a value bias in our choice of indicators of disparity. Matthews gives the example of residents of Atlantic Canada who may be seen either as disadvantaged or advantaged in terms of their housing, depending upon whether the average number of people per unit (high-disadvantaged) or the proportion of home owners (high-advantaged) is used as a marker. An evaluation of the advantages and disadvantages of rural life has mostly been made from an urban point of view.

Throughout this discussion of rural traditions in Canada, neither "elderly" or "aging" has been defined. Canadian definitions of the elderly have developed in an urban milieu, associated with institutionalized ages of passage from work to retirement and of eligibility for social security benefits such as Old Age Security. For many years it has been accepted that age 65 marks the entry to old age. This marker may change in the future. The Canadian Charter of Rights and Freedoms, R.S.C. 1985, Appendix 2, No. 44, has opened to question the issue of the mandatory age of retirement, so that 65 may no longer be the predictable age of exit from the labour force.

As the discussion in this chapter has indicated, rural elders were traditionally involved in primary industries that had no established age of retirement. People worked as long as their health permitted; needs of subsequent generations and income requirements were more likely than age to be determinants of retirement. If a rural bartender at age 78 is still doing the same things as he always has done, in terms of functional age, he is ageless (Adams, 1975). In rural areas, age may be a matter of how well one continues to cope with one's environment. Because of urban conventions and the predisposition of researchers to use age 65 as the beginning of old age, much of the discussion in this book will, by necessity use these same indicators. An attempt is also made to look at some of the variations throughout the country in what it means to be old and in how age affects work status, health and family interaction.

OUTLINE OF THE BOOK

In susequent chapters of the book, several major topics concerning the lives of contemporary rural seniors in Canada are addressed. Chapter 2 includes a discussion of patterns of work and retirement of farm and non-farm seniors. An analysis of leisure patterns of those in the post-retirement years highlights the difficulties in determining what is leisure among a group of people who are work oriented. Some of the environmental determinants of the abilities of rural seniors to live independently are discussed in Chapter 3. These include housing and facilities such as, for example, electricity and water. In Chapter 4, a discussion of family networks, support, and interaction addresses the question of the interdependence of rural families. Chapter 5 is an analysis of health status and attitudes toward health of rural seniors and the place of health promotion in developing health programs in rural areas. In Chapter 6 research, policy and service directions are proposed.

Throughout the book Canadian data are used when possible. Comparisons are made with other western countries although direct comparisons are difficult because of the variations in the census definitions of "rural".

CHAPTER 2

WORK, RETIREMENT AND LEISURE

WORK

The occupational definition of rural, which divides residents into farm and non-farm categories, emerged from the agricultural history of rural Canada discussed in the previous chapter. The hard, physical labour involved in farming led to the development of a strong work ethic in rural communities and activities that did not involve physical labour were not seen as 'real' work. In the absence of social security and mandatory retirement, people worked for as long as possible. Leisure was to be avoided, for to be caught 'loafing' was cause for embarrassment (Bauder and Doerflinger, 1967).

In the late twentieth century, only some of these traditions are evident in the patterns of work, retirement and leisure of rural elders. Most rural residents now work in non-farm occupations, although rural seniors are still more likely than urban seniors to remain in the work force. Farmers tend to work until late in life, and the continued participation of rural seniors in the labour force seems to be encouraged by financial necessity which comes from a lifetime of low income, lack of pension and underemployment.

Retirement of self-employed rural seniors is a long, gradual process which occurs later than for urban residents. This retirement tradition comes from farm retirement which is based on family transfer of land. Little is known about retirement of rural employees or about the post-retirement adjustment of those who retire to the countryside. Attitudes to leisure and leisure activities of rural seniors are relatively unexplored, although there is little evidence that leisure is considered unacceptable.

The purpose of this chapter is to discuss the scope of labour force involvement of rural seniors and to consider the relatively new phenomenon of rural retirement. High rates of labour-force participation on the part of rural seniors are discussed in the context of rural ideologies about work. Research on retirement is reviewed and the conclusion drawn that little is known about retirement of the non-farm rural resident. Leisure activities of rural seniors are considered in light of the assumption that leisure may be devalued among those who hold a traditional rural ideology of hard work.

Labour Force Participation of Older Workers

Among contemporary Canadians, there are no overall differences in types of occupations of urban and rural non-farm residents (Statistics Canada, 1984a). Despite the argument that the only 'real' work of rural residents is the physical labour required in primary industries, the range of jobs done by rural residents is now just as great as that of urban dwellers. One vestige of the stereotype of rural work as "real work" does remain. Most of the people who do the physical work in primary industries are rural dwellers.

With the exception of rural farm residents, gender is a more important determinant of occupation than rural or urban residence. Canadian women are most represented in clerical, service, sales, teaching medicine and other health care jobs. With the exception of farm-women, urban and rural women are employed in similar proportions in these occupations. Men are most represented in managerial, administrative, construction, product fabricating, service and sales occupations. Again, with the exception of farming, urban and rural men are employed in similar proportions in these occupations (Statistics Canada, 1984a).

Differences do emerge, however, when one considers older workers in primary industries. Over 75 percent of older workers are in agricultural, service and trade occupations (Canada, 1982). In Canada, farming is now an occupation of older workers. Farm men over age 55 make up 65 percent of all farmers and farmers have the highest average age (49) of all occupational groups in Canada (Statistics Canada 1984a). Of older women involved in primary occupations, the largest proportion (65 percent) are in farm-support jobs including farm and nursery work. Married women-farmers tend to be placed in this category since they are more often designated as farm-workers and their husbands as farmers (Lee, 1987). The second largest group (32 percent) of older women in primary occupations is farmers. This group is largely made up of older women who are farm owners because of widowhood. In contrast to farming, fishing, forestry and mining are occupations of younger workers. Less than 6 percent of men and 1 percent of women over 55 are involved in these jobs (Statistics Canada, 1984a).

Among older workers in Canada, the occupational designation of rural as farm versus non-farm still has some utility since most of the current cohort of older rural workers are in farming. However, overall, work patterns of rural residents suggest that the focus on farming as the major rural occupation will soon be inappropriate. As older farmers retire, their land is often sold and developed for non-agricultural purposes and so the range of occupations of rural workers is becoming even broader. The current occupational designation ignores the variety of occupations of rural residents and might best be abandoned in favour of a full list of occupations similar to that for urban workers.

Rates of Labour Force Participation

A basic element of the rural ideology discussed in Chapter 1 is a strong work ethic. Rates of labour-force participation provide some information about commitment to work; one indictor of a strong work ethic being high levels of labour-force activity.

Of Canadians over 65 who remain in the workforce, the majority have no employer-sponsored pensions (McDonald and Wanner, 1989), and many are self-employed. Farmers over age 65 have dramatically higher labour-force involvement than either urban or non-farm seniors. The majority of older farmers are in the labour-force. Rural women are employed at lower rates than men, but in the same relative proportions **(Table 2.1)**.

One question concerning labour-force participation of farm seniors is whether they continue to work because of a positive work commitment or because of a lack of alternative means of support. Self employment allows rural seniors to continue working as long as they wish and are able to do so (Mark, 1981). However, employment after age 60 does not lead to higher income (Martin Matthews, 1988a). A Saskatchewan survey of needs of the elderly (Senior Citizens Provincial Council, 1987) showed that 41 percent of urban elders received the Guaranteed Income Supplement as compared to 60 percent of rural elders. This suggests that for many rural elders, employment is less a matter of choice than of necessity.

Differences in employment patterns by marital status provide some support for the idea that need is the basis of labour-force attachment **(Table 2.1)**. Single women are more likely than married women to be employed, presumably because they must be self-supporting. Widowed and divorced farm women are likely to be running their farm operations and hence have higher rates of employment than others who are widowed or divorced. Overall, higher unemployment among rural than urban women suggests a greater difficulty faced by rural women in finding employment.

Employment rates do not vary by marital status for men. However, single urban men and single non-farm men report the highest rates of unemployment. Farm men report no unemployment because of the opportunities provided by self-employment to remain in the labour force.

Although rural residents may retain work for economic reasons, those who have retired appear relatively satisfied with their economic status. A comparison of urban and rural retirees in the vicinity of Kitchener, Ontario, found that more rural (79 percent) than urban (61 percent) retirees thought their retirement incomes were adequate. In fact, 70 percent of rural and 48 percent of urban retirees considered themselves to be in an equal or better financial situation than they were before retirement (Brown and Martin Matthews, 1981). Neither low income nor perceived economic deprivation were predictors of post-retirement employment. The authors concluded

TABLE 2.1

LABOUR FORCE ACTIVITY OF OLDER WORKERS OVER AGE 65 BY GENDER AND MARITAL STATUS RURAL/URBAN, FARM/NON-FARM

	Participation Rate[1]			Unemployment Rate[2]		
	Total	Male	Female	Total	Male	Female
Urban						
Total 65 and over	8	13	5	4	4	4
Single	14	13	15	6	16	2
Married	10	14	4	4	3	6
Widowed and						
Divorced	5	8	4	4	4	4
Rural						
Total 65 and over	14	22	6	2	2	4
Single	20	24	12	2	2	2
Married	16	23	5	2	2	5
Widowed and						
Divorced	8	15	6	3	3	4
Farm						
Total 65 and over	57	83	19	0	0	1
Single	65	75	25	0	0	0
Married	63	89	16	0	0	1
Widowed and						
Divorced	34	57	22	1	0	1
Non-farm						
Total 65 and over	8	12	4	4	4	5
Single	12	12	11	4	6	2
Married	9	13	4	4	4	7
Widowed and						
Divorced	5	9	4	5	5	5

SOURCE: Statistics Canada, (1984c) *Population Labour Force Activity.* Catalogue # 92-915, Table 1.
[1] Participation rate is total employed over total population in that age category.
[2] Unemployed rate is total unemployed over total labour force in that age category.

that employment satisfies some personal needs but is apparently not used to satisfy economic needs (Snell and Brown, 1987).

It is not clear whether self employment is the major variable explaining the difference in employment patterns of older rural and urban workers. There have been few studies comparing self-employed people in these settings. Nor have marital status, gender and other economic factors been fully explored as possible factors in explaining different employment patterns of rural and urban workers.

The situations of Ruth and Al Wilson as summarized in Chapter 1, illustrate some of the unexplored questions concerning labour-force participation and work commitment of rural seniors. Neither Ruth nor Al are now involved in the labour force, although both have indexed pensions from their previous jobs and are able to afford a high standard of living in Kaslo. They hold a privileged position compared to Murray Nelson. Both had satisfying and stimulating jobs. Both were able to choose the timing and location of their retirement. They have more than sufficient income to enjoy chosen activities in retirement. Murray Nelson may choose to continue farming but like other farmers he may resent the assumptions of urban people that the farming life is restful and idyllic. It is just as likely that Murray continues to work because he has no pension and no outside interests . His 'town' job not only provides an income but a social setting as well.

Barriers to Labour Force Participation

Labour-force activity is one indicator of work commitment. The self-employed have the advantage of having no mandatory retirement, but their continued participation in the labour-force after the age of 65 is not necessarily due to the fact that they place a high value on work. Many of these older self-employed workers may nevertheless be forced out of the work-force involuntarily by age 65 (Gunn, Verkley and Newman, 1983) because they cannot compete successfully for jobs due to age discrimination and rapid technological change.

These general employment problems faced by the older worker may be exacerbated for those living in rural areas. For women, greater distances from employment opportunities mean longer travelling time and less time available for required household duties. Low levels of services in rural areas remove a possible source of employment in the service sector. Rural ideologies in which women are expected to be available if their husbands need them and community sanctions against working off the farm inhibit employment opportunities for farm women (Gasson, 1984; Keating, Doherty, and Munro, 1987).

Barriers to employment for rural men are somewhat different than they are for women. Among farm men, there is little unemployment, and most work into their late 60s. However, opportunities to work in other resource industries are restricted to younger men. While the average age of men in farming is 49, the average age of men in mining is only 34. Unemployment rates of older non-farm men are substantially higher than those of farm men (**Table 2.1**), indicating that the former group is disadvantaged in its access to employment.

One employment pattern not evident from labour force statistics is that of part-time employment which can be part of a lifelong pattern of seasonal or part-time work. Many rural communities have chronic underemployment because of the nature of local work opportunities. In the mining and tourist community of Kaslo, British Columbia, only 45 percent of all male workers and 29 percent of all female workers have full-time jobs (Statistics Canada, 1988a). In the fishing village of Clark's Harbour, Nova Scotia, there are even fewer full-time employees: 30 percent of men and 18 percent of women (Statistics Canada, 1988b). In the farming community of Plaisance, Quebec, 68 percent of men and 44 percent of women work full-time (Statistics Canada, 1988c). Although we know that many older workers are employed part-time (Senior Citizens Provincial Council, 1983), we do not know how many have always worked this way. Chronic underemployment must surely affect seniors' attitudes toward work and retirement from work.

In summary, older rural workers are likely to face three types of barriers to employment: rural beliefs that exclude women from employment; lack of employment opportunities in sparsely populated areas, and lack of access to jobs in resource industries other than farming. These barriers are different than those faced by urban workers who are more likely to confront compulsory retirement policies and a competitive work force. Nonetheless, employment barriers seem likely to increase with the decrease in numbers of people involved in farming. One of the problems that may arise from these changes is an increased difference in financial status between urban in-migrants who are likely to move to rural areas with more financial assets, and their rural contemporaries who may have had a lifetime of low income or chronic underemployment.

Retirement from Work

Although farming has traditionally been considered the primary rural occupation, rural residents are involved in a great variety of types of work. However, because of the focus on farming, and because farming is unique to the rural setting, more is known about farm retirement than about retirement from other rural jobs. No one has addressed the question of whether retirement from teaching or clerical work is a different experience for rural than urban residents.

To understand differences in types of rural retirement, it is useful to divide rural work into two categories: self-employed and employee. Farmers are the major group of self-employed workers in rural areas, although there are many others in such diverse occupations as equipment sales, pharmacy and restaurant ownership. Retirement from self-employment is usually a lengthy process, sometimes occurring over several years (Keating and Marshall, 1980). In contrast to the self-employed, most rural workers are employees of large or small businesses. For them, retirement is often a single event or rite of passage (McDonald and Wanner, 1989).

Retirement as an Event

Studies of the retirment of rural employees have focused on the timing, symbolic importance and influence of retirement as these differ between rural and urban environments. In a comparative study of urban and rural retirees in the area of Kitchener, Ontario, Brown and Martin Matthews (1981) found no rural-urban differences in timing of retirement. Almost half of both rural and urban residents retired before they were 65 and the majority of both groups said their retirement was voluntary. Most gave poor health, company policy or job-related reasons for retirement. These findings provide no evidence of a stronger work ethic among rural than urban workers.

There has been some speculation that the event of retirement has little symbolic importance in the lives of retirees (McDonald and Wanner, 1989). Findings from a study by Martin Matthews et al. (1982) suggest that this may well be the case. In a study of 300 retired men and women living in southern Ontario, the authors developed a life events scale in which respondents generated and then ranked the impact of life events, including retirement. Of 34 life events, retirement ranked 28th in importance, suggesting that it is not a critical life event.

In contrast, the event of retirement has been shown to have special meaning to farmers (Selles and Keating, 1989). Retirement from an off-farm job was considered a normal event. However, retirement from farming was seen as a negative event, imposed on those unfortunate enough to have ill health, to be forced to sell the farm or to be unable to get along with children who had taken over the operation. Farmers saw the last phase of their own work-lives as one in which they were 'semi-retired' and still involved in some of the day-to-day operation of the farm.

Research on the rituals surrounding retirement in rural communities might prove useful in understanding the symbolic nature of the event. In farm families one of the common events associated with the transfer of operation of the business from one generation to the next is the changing of residences on the farm. Often this means that the younger generation move into the 'big house' and the older couple move into a smaller house on the property. This type of event may have a different meaning than the party or gift given to the retiring employee.

Because there is so little research on the retirement of rural employees, it is premature to speculate on the importance of retirement to these rural dwellers. However, it may be useful to consider the impact of the wage labour economy in rural Canada. In some parts of the country, wage labour is a new phenomenon. The introduction of wage labour into the Arctic has recently created retirement as a rite of passage in an environment where there was previously no such concept (McClelland and Miles, 1987). As a result, many people in the western Arctic have adapted their lifestyles and aspirations to the income wage–labour produced. One tangible result has been increased demand for consumer goods and the emergence of a devalued status among those who cannot purchase those goods: the retired and the unemployed. Retirement emerged as an abrupt event defined by exit from wage–labour rather than as a gradual process associated with biological aging. Prior to the introduction of wage-labour, men and women became old and moved into 'retirement' by virtue of an inability to do certain kinds of work (Guemple, 1980). For men, this occurred when they could no longer hunt on a year-round basis and began to pass on the task of hunting for the family's food to younger men in the household. For women, work tasks were more varied and somewhat less strenuous so that advancing age was not so limiting.

Wage–labour is now well established in most parts of rural Canada, ensuring that the majority of future retirees will be employees who will have a defined retirement event. Changes in the nature of work and retirement in the Arctic provide only one example of the potential impact on rural communities of this shift. Further research on the nature of rural retirement will help determine both its symbolic meaning and its effect on rural communities as these communities move away from an agricultural base.

Retirement as a Process

Retirement as a process is usually approached from the perspective of how an individual relinquishes the employment or work role and acquires and then perhaps relinquishes the retirement role. There are relatively few process models of retirement. Atchely's (1983) much-quoted model has two pre-retirement and five post-retirement stages, all in anticipation of, or in response to, the retirement event. Entry into the process begins with anticipation of the event and includes remote and near phases. Post-event phases include honeymoon, disenchantment, reorientation, stability and termination. Termination can occur through the acquisition of another role such as that of worker, widow or invalid. Unfortunately, this model has been little tested so that it is difficult to determine its utility.

The investigation of the process of retirement of rural residents has been almost entirely focused on farmers who have no prescribed retirement event. In a study of 315 older farmers in Alberta, Keating and Munro (1989) proposed a model of the retirement process which included a sequence of exit from the farm business. They found that the order of exit was:

farmwork, livestock holdings, production management, marketing management, financial management, land holdings and equipment holdings. The exit process began with a reduction in work when the farmer was in his early 50s, and extended to his 70s or beyond before the final transfer of ownership. The order of exit from the business was one of decreasing control over the operation. Reduction in work brings little loss of business control. In fact, it may increase control if work is passed on to younger family members as part of their socialization into the business. Management control is reduced gradually, with major decisions relinquished last. Ownership is the last phase of exit from the business. Not only does ownership provide the legal right to control over the business, it also conveys the status of farmer.

Some process models of retirement from farming include a focus on both the retiring and receiving generations. In a qualitative study of a farming community in northern Alberta, Selles (1988) found that partial retirement occurred when sons were young adults still living at home. During this stage, the son took on more fieldwork, was consulted on management decisions and became 'interested and involved with the father'. Semi-retirement occurred when the son married, some property was transferred to him, and he assumed management responsibility. The father assisted in some farm chores, worked at peak times of the year such as planting and was 'interested and involved with the son'. The final stage is complete retirement, often seen by the farmer as forced and undesirable. During this final stage there may be some evidence of the farmer's disapproval of his enforced idleness.

Process models of rural retirees have, to date, been rather narrowly focused on one group of rural residents, male farmers. Little is known about the retirement of other rural groups, of women, or of those who retire from both self-employment and wage-labour. The models developed for farmers suggest that the process of retirement spans many years and is interdependent with both business and family cycles. Farming requires an especially complex retirement process since work and family are so closely interrelated. Not only do family members work together but they live at their place of business. Few other self employed workers are in the same situation. More common is the situation of family members, such as in a family restaurant, working together but living at a distance. Other groups of self-employed professionals, such as, for example, dentists and pharmacists, have neither co-workers who are kin, nor residence at the place of work. For these groups retirement has fewer family implications and is more likely to be an individual process, dependent on such factors as the availability of other professionals to buy the business. A further exploration of business, personal and family interrelationships is warranted in the study of rural retirement.

Post-Retirement Adjustment

Lack of research interest in the retirement of rural workers has meant that there is little information on subsequent adjustment to the loss of the work role. Most post-retirement research has been limited to an examination of lifestyle decisions made by rural retirees. Much of this research has been on mobility: in and out-movers to rural areas, adjustment of in-movers to the rural milieu and an exploration of the reasons why retirees remain in resource towns that have gone bust.

One study that provides some evidence of post-retirement adjustment of older rural adults is an analysis of moving intentions of a group of pre-retired and recently-retired men living in villages in central Alberta (Keating and Brundin, 1983). All of the men had been self-employed, half in farming and half in other businesses. Those who were considering moving in the near future were men who had children at the launching stage and who were recently-retired. Launching of children prompts consideration of moving because of changes in household structure, while retirement provides the freedom to consider a move to another location. Anticipated moves at this stage were seen positively. However, anticipation of future moves was viewed more negatively and was seen as something that might be imposed by negative changes in health status. Types of moves expected at this later stage were into congregate housing such as lodges and nursing homes. There was no association between type of occupation (farm versus non-farm) and consideration of moving.

Moving intentions related to retirement do not necessarily correlate with actual mobility, even from undesirable locations. High rates of out-migration are expected from 'boom towns' since they tend to have little economic base and few services, once resource extraction has been completed. Stafford (1984) surveyed 364 retirees in one such group of 16 small towns in northwestern Ontario. The towns had populations of 1000 to 4000 and had been dominated by pulp and paper mills and mining of gold, copper and iron. Stafford hypothesized that a large proportion of recent retirees would leave for other places with lower costs of living, more amenities and more moderate climates. However, he found that retirees were not geographically mobile and preferred to stay in familiar surroundings, perhaps because of a strong attachment to place or because of the anticipated cost and disruption of long-distance moves.

Low degrees of mobility are typical of both rural and urban seniors. As a group, rural residents over age 65 are least likely to move, indicating a somewhat stronger attachment to place by rural than urban dwellers. However, exit from the labour force appears to have a differential influence on mobility, depending on age. Rural residents over age 65 are not mobile regardless of whether they are part of the labour force. However, younger rural residents (aged 55-64) are much more likely to be mobile if they are not part of the labour force. This latter group is partly made up of those who retire to rural communities, like Ruth Wilson who was described in Chapter 1. Many retired in-migrants to rural areas come with relatively recession-proof pensions (Cook, 1987) which allow for early retirement and a choice of retirement location.

As indicated by this review of retirement adjustment and activities, little is known about how rural retirees adapt to the absence of the work role. There is evidence that, like urban retirees, rural residents tend not to be geographically mobile, although there has been no Canadian research on the impact on rural areas of urban retirees who settle there.

The heterogeneity of work patterns of rural workers requires a broadening of our investigations into rural retirement. We have yet to determine the importance of the rural environment in determining patterns of work and retirement. While Ruth and Al Wilson made a distinct shift in activity and location when they retired, Murray Nelson has had no such shift in work-life or in location. Retirement may be much less important to him than urban research would suggest. Nor do we know if urban and rural retirement are similar for those in the same types of jobs, such as teaching or clerical work. It is time to compare the process of retirement, retirement adjustment and post-retirement mobility of men and women holding similar jobs in urban and rural settings.

Although there is evidence that the timing, meaning and process of retirement are different for farmers than for those who are not self-employed, we have insufficient data to know whether other self-employed groups operate in the same manner. Rural communities are made up of large numbers of self-employed people who are not involved in agriculture. The cultural milieu of work and retirement also deserves some special consideration. The shift of native people toward wage economies means that more rural seniors will experience a transition from employment to retirement.

LEISURE

The history of rural Canada, with its heavy emphasis on work as a matter of survival and as a means to status in the community, hardly seems likely to have created a milieu in which a high value would be placed on leisure activities, especially sedentary, non-productive activities. Yet, the fact that the rural lifestyle typically has been one of heavy work-loads, should mean that there is a great deal of additional time available for leisure to those rural residents who have retired from work. Retired people are estimated to have twice as much leisure time in an average day as do those who are working (Novak, 1985).

There are several hypotheses concerning the relationship between leisure and work, most based on the tenet that the type and amount of work determines the amount of time available for leisure and the appropriate leisure activities (McPherson, 1990). The three most common interpretations of the work-leisure relationship are: spillover/congruence, compensation/contrast and neutrality/segmentation (Zuzanek and Mannell, 1983).

Leisure in the Rural Setting

Most of the evidence of the relationship between work and leisure of rural seniors suggests that leisure activities spill over from previous work activities. The spillover hypothesis is that people carry their skills and attitudes from one domain to the next. Since work is a centrally important life-activity for most people, work affects leisure (Zuzanek and Mannell, 1983).

There are no reported differences in the overall levels of activity of rural and urban seniors (Strain and Chappell, 1982). However, relationships between work and leisure may be different for urban and rural dwellers. Shamir and Ruskin (1983) undertook a rural-urban comparison of 81 kibbutz and 81 urban residents. They hypothesized that work would be more important to kibbutz dwellers than urban dwellers and that rural-urban differences would emerge because, in the rural kibbutz, work and leisure were more interrelated. They found that kibbutz residents did not define themselves more strongly through work than did urban residents. However, they did find confirmation for the idea that the structure of the community is important in determining the relationship between work and leisure. Only in the more segregated urban environment did they find evidence of compensation in work and leisure. This is a second hypothesis about the work-leisure relationship, that leisure compensates for elements of life that are missing on the job (Zuzanek and Mannell, 1983). In a closed community such as the kibbutz, spillover from work to leisure was most likely because of the close connections between work and leisure.

These findings have ramifications for Canadian rural dwellers who live in integrated settings. Long-time residents in small rural communities such as Newfoundland fishing villages or prairie farming communities, may find little opportunity in their near-environments to pursue compensatory leisure activities. One way in which rural dwellers may solve this problem is to redefine the boundaries of their community. In a study of farmer couples in central Alberta, Grudinzki and Passmore (1988) found that the leisure community was far away for many farmers. One farmer was very involved in competitive trap shooting and the people with whom he competed lived all over the province. Another couple was involved in amateur theatre in the nearest town which was 40 km away.

The work-leisure relationship may be different in rural areas than it is in urban areas because of the relatively high proportion of rural self-employed and because of the integrated nature of many rural communities. The example of the farmer involved in trap-shooting suggests that it is difficult for farmers to find activities that contrast with their daily work. This may be more generally true in small rural communities that have few organized leisure activities that would allow the participant to take part in leisure that is unrelated to work. Spillover from current or former work activities seems likely among those who are self-employed and live in small integrated rural communities. This idea remains untested.

Leisure Activities

The most frequent type of survey of seniors in rural areas is that which documents the level and type of recreational and leisure activities pursued. Most studies of leisure activities of rural seniors are descriptive and do not address the question of the relationship between work and leisure. By implication, this research suggests segmentation of these two facets of life.

Much of the data on leisure activities suggest that rural seniors are sedentary. Television watching is the most common leisure activity for both community-dwelling and institutionalized elders (Hodge, 1984; Humboldt Community Survey Committee, 1976), although community dwellers have

TABLE 2.2

PERCENTAGE OF PEOPLE INVOLVED IN PHYSICAL ACTIVITY BY GENDER AND AGE

Level of Activity

Age	N	Sedentary[1]		Moderate[2]		Active[3]	
		M	F	M	F	M	F
14-19	2,736	5	5	22	24	73	71
20-24	2,365	4	7	33	35	63	57
25-34	4,495	5	9	39	39	55	53
35-44	3,051	8	12	42	38	50	50
45-54	2,372	12	14	42	36	46	50
55-64	2,107	15	16	36	30	49	54
65-74	1,614	17	21	26	27	56	52
75+	842	26	34	22	17	52	50

SOURCE: McPherson, B.D. and C.A. Kozlik (1987). "Age Patterns in Leisure Participation: The Canadian Case". In V. Marshall (ed.), *Aging in Canada: Social Perspectives.* Markham, Ontario: Fitzhenry and Whiteside, p. 219.

[1] Sedentary: less than three hours of physical activity per week for less than nine months per year.
[2] Moderate: less than three hours of physical activity per week for at least nine months per year, or an average of at least three hours of physical activity per week for less than nine months per year.
[3] Active: an average of at least three hours of physical activity per week, for at least nine months a year.

a larger range of activities such as handicrafts, visiting and volunteer work. In her research on seniors in Nova Scotia, Fiaz (1983: 89) notes that "[i]nactivity, and perhaps social apathy of the institutionalized individuals stands in sharp contrast with the zest for living shown by the remainder of the retired individuals". Such observations highlight the need to go beyond lists of leisure activities to the meanings of those activities in the lives of participants. While television watching may be central to those who do not have the health or opportunity for other activities, it may serve as a contrast to those with more broadly based leisure experiences.

One of the most consistent findings in the literature on leisure of older adults is that older Canadians are less physically active than are younger Canadians (McPherson, 1986). Findings from the Canada Fitness Survey of 22,000 Canadians, indicate that the general decline in active fitness only holds true up to age 55 (McPherson and Kozlik, 1987). Approximately half of the respondents in each age group over age 55 were involved in three hours of physical activity per week (**Table 2.2**). However, there is more variety in the amount of physical activity among the older age groups than any other group, with almost half of respondents over age 55 being either sedentary or moderate in their activity. While almost equal proportions of men and women of all ages are active, larger percentages of older women than men are sedentary.

Findings from the Public Opinion Survey on Recreation (Alberta Recreation and Parks. 1984a) also show that some seniors are physically active. Approximately 23 percent of seniors in the survey were from rural areas, although data were not analyzed for rural-urban comparisons. Seventy percent of the seniors surveyed participated in some form of outdoor activity. Most (62 percent) were involved in walking for pleasure, with a few involved in organized sports such as golf (26 percent), bowling (13 percent) and curling (11 percent). Higher percentages of senior Albertans than any other age group were involved in sports and outdoor activities. Patterns of recreational activities are also changing, with increases in hiking, cycling, cross-country skiing and water-based activities among seniors. Nonetheless, the likelihood of starting a new activity is lower among seniors (37 percent) than it is for younger cohorts (48 percent).

Heterogeneity in Leisure Activities

The last section suggests that seniors are not homogeneous in their level of leisure involvement. In the last few years, leisure researchers have also begun to acknowledge the heterogeneity of the elderly in terms of their range of leisure activities. Types of leisure activity pursued vary by culture, by geographical remoteness, by age and by rural-urban location.

For instance, seniors living in remote areas may prefer social and leisure activities that are different from those preferred by seniors living in less remote, small communities. Findings from a study of the needs of seniors in the Peace River district of northern Alberta (Peace River Health Unit, 1986) illustrate some of these differences.

The Peace River Health Unit has a population of 40,000 living in an area of 27,500 square miles. There are six small towns in the area. The majority of seniors living in the most remote parts of the area were native Canadians. Those in remote areas had lower levels of interest in all leisure activities (visiting, cultural recreation, physical recreation, planning senior services and volunteer work) than those in less remote areas. Native seniors did not participate in senior centres even when such centres were nearby. More seniors in the remote areas lived in extended family settings, perhaps reducing the need to visit with others or to meet younger people. Distance from activities, transportation problems and language barriers may also have reduced interest. Many native seniors and those of other ethnic backgrounds did not read or speak English, the language of most seniors' organizations and the language of other formal activities. A generally lower standard of living in remote areas also meant that more time had to be spent on maintenance activities. Many had no running water, plumbing or central heating.

Seniors in other remote areas also have low levels of involvement in leisure activities. Only 18 percent of a sample of Newfoundland and Labrador seniors living in remote areas said that they engaged in recreational activities such as crafts and/or hobbies (Vivian, 1982). These two studies suggest that those living in remote areas with few services and low levels of resources and amenities do not see organized leisure activities as relevant to them. One reason for this finding is pragmatic; if amenities are unavailable because of language barriers or distance, they will not be used. Also, rural-urban comparisons of types of preferred leisure activities show that rural residents are more likely to be involved in land-based activities such as fishing that do not require organized facilities, while urban residents are more likely to be involved in facility-based activities such as racquet sports and going to movies (Alberta Recreation and Parks, 1984b).

In the past few years researchers have also begun to look at activity patterns among seniors of different age cohorts. Studies in a rural retirement community in Ontario (Break, 1985) and of seniors in Newfoundland and Labrador, have shown that age is negatively related to amount of recreational activity. More attention needs to be paid to differences in the leisure involvement of various age cohorts of seniors. Although older seniors are likely to be in poorer health than those who are younger, attitudes toward leisure may also influence recreational choices among different cohorts.

It seems likely that our understanding of the relationship between work and leisure suffers from an urban bias. Rural seniors living in remote areas do not separate work from family or leisure and the concept of leisure may simply not be relevant to them. Even those living in small communities such as Kaslo may have little experience of incorporating leisure into their lives. A person like Murray Nelson who comes from an impoverished background and has always held two jobs, may not see a place for leisure in his life. In contrast, Ruth and Al Wilson, who have retired from a major metropolitan area, have always had access to organized leisure activities and have had jobs with defined work and non-work time.

Findings from research on leisure activities of rural seniors suggest that rather than spillover or compensation, most leisure activities of rural residents support the neutrality or segmentation hypothesis; i.e., any relationship between work and leisure is coincidental (Zuzanek and Mannell, 1983). Activities may be unrelated to work because they are influenced by the physical environment more than by work. Thus, those living in rural areas have easy access to outdoor recreation while those in urban areas use available facilities. The variety of work and living situations of rural elders influences their attitudes toward leisure and their choice of leisure activities. In recent decades, researchers have begun to document some of these differences and to test hypotheses concerning the relationship between work and leisure. A useful extension of this research would be to systematically test the influence of rural variables such as, for example, proximity to lakes and mountains, on meanings of leisure and type and degree of involvement in leisure activities.

Interventions to Change Activity/Fitness Levels

Increasing the level of physical activity of older adults is currently seen as a goal by leisure theorists and practitioners. McPherson (1988:94) muses about "how I could both instruct and convince gerontologists that regular physical activity is a necessary ingredient to achieve one's potential throughout the life course, regardless of age." However, he also warns that "[w]ith the growth of the fitness and wellness movements, entrepreneurs in the private sector and disciples of the various movements, generated many unsubstantiated beliefs that extolled the physiological and psychological benefits of fitness programs for middle-aged and older adults" (McPherson, 1988: 105).

Despite such warnings, many reports of the levels of physical activity of rural seniors suggest that researchers assume that seniors should be doing much more. When less than 10 percent of seniors in a study in Antigonish, Nova Scotia participated in fun and fitness classes, Fiaz (1983) seemed concerned that such activities remain the purvue of the young and middle aged. An unanswered question in the study is whether lack of interest in fitness classes comes from disinterest in all physical activity or reluctance to take on a new activity.

There has been only a small amount of research on programs structured to change levels of physical activity and physical fitness of older people. One approach was taken by Cunningham, Rechnitzer and Donner (1986). They suggested that self-paced walking is a reasonable measure of age-related 'slowing down' and may be a useful measure of fitness. Their research was an experimental design in which they measured the effect of exercise training on walking speed. Subjects, including a control group, were measured at the beginning of the experiment and again, one year later. The intervention was walking or jogging for 30 minutes, three times a week for one year. After one year the training group had significantly increased their normal walking speed. "The self-selected walking pace could eventually prove to be an adequate measure of cardiovascular fitness and physical activity among the elderly. This technique may prove useful as a screening device in assessing cardiovascular fitness for older subjects unable or unwilling to walk on a treadmill or ride a cycle ergometer" (1986: 25).

Stones, Kozma and Stones (1985) evaluated the effects of a more general fitness program called the 3F program (Fitness with Fun and Fellowship for the over Fifties), conducted in St. John's, Newfoundland. This program includes two weekly, 45 – minute sessions with opportunities for swimming, square dancing, Tai Chi and social events. The membership in the program was 400, with a mean age in the early 60s. The authors found an association between happiness, low levels of anxiety and duration of physical activity. Longitudinal analyses indicated that physical activity may help offset decline in reaction time associated with age.

Until there are more data on the positive effects of increased physical activity, it remains a matter of opinion whether the activity levels of rural seniors are too low. Both research on cardiovascular fitness and on the psychological advantages of regular fitness activities are promising starts in providing information to test the assumption.

Adoption of Leisure Activities

One of the difficulties in developing intervention programs to increase levels of activity of rural seniors is that there has been little systematic review of factors that influence the adoption of leisure activities or pursuits. At this stage of life, factors such as place of residence, ethnicity, age and social group may be more important than relationships to work in determining approaches to leisure (McPherson, 1990; Staines, 1980). Yet, if leisure is a major part of retirement, and if factors affecting choice of leisure activities are different after retirement, one would expect some post-retirement change in leisure pursuits. Evidence to date suggests that few people actually adopt new activities in retirement.

An understanding of the circumstances under which rural seniors will take part in leisure activities could be useful to programmers developing activity programs for rural residents, for policy-makers determining how municipal funds will be allocated to the construction of recreation facilities, and to leisure researchers to illustrate areas in which there are gaps in the conceptual understanding of the adoption of leisure activities. In order to understand how rural seniors adopt leisure activities, the model developed by Brandenburg et al. (1982) will be used (Figure 2.1).

According to Brandenburg et al., the process of adoption of leisure activities begins with the individual's preoccupations and interests and ends with adoption of an activity if certain conditions are met. These conditions include opportunity, knowledge, favourable social milieu and receptiveness.

Opportunity

Opportunity requires the presence of favourable conditions in the near environment and the absence of constraints. Such things as geographic accessibility, availability of transportation, physical capabilities, financial

FIGURE 2.1

A CONCEPTUAL MODEL OF THE RECREATIONAL ACTIVITY ADOPTION PROCESS

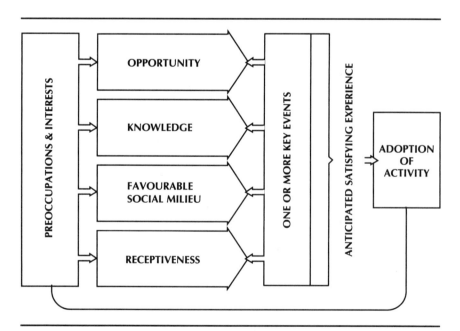

SOURCE: Brandenburg et. al. (1982). A Conceptual Model of How People Adopt Recreation Activities. *Leisure Studies* 1:269, Figure 1.

considerations and time, determine opportunity. In a study of the recreational activities of seniors in two rural Manitoba communities, Strain and Chappell (1982) found that opportunities to take part in leisure activities were not related to level of involvement. When comparing two rural communities, the authors found no differences in rates of participation, although one of the communities was far better served with recreational facilities. When asked why they did not participate in activities, the most frequent reasons given by respondents were lack of facilities (36 percent), time constraints (17 percent), health (14 percent) and transportation problems (4 percent). Though important, opportunity is not a sufficient reason for adoption of an activity.

Hiltner, Smith and Sullivan (1986) addressed the question of relative availability of recreational facilities by comparing service utilization by a sample of 149 urban and 162 rural elders in northwestern Ohio. They found that the overall utilization rate of social and recreational services was 35 percent for both groups. The authors suggest that the specific rural area in which the research was conducted may account for the lack of difference between rural and urban seniors. "Because the rural road network is extensive, incomes are adequate, and most of the elderly worked in nearby cities and towns rather than on farms prior to retirement, their service usage patterns may not significantly differ from the patterns of the urban elderly" (Hiltner, Smith and Sullivan, 1986: 239). Rural and urban seniors appeared to have similar opportunities to take part in recreation and most (62 percent) respondents felt no need for additional services.

Knowledge

Knowledge about an activity is the second condition of its adoption. People gain knowledge through prior experience with the activity, by having read or been told about it, or by seeing a demonstration. McPherson (1978) makes the point that the current cohort of seniors was not socialized to include physical activity as part of their repertoire of leisure activities. Age-based norms which discourage involvement in physical activities may preclude the development of knowledge about an activity.

Social Milieu

The third condition is the social milieu in which a person lives. People in one's social milieu must be seen to accept the activity. The movement into a new activity may require a new social environment consistent with that activity. For example, the Seniors Games are associated with small groups of very active, physically fit seniors in small towns and rural communities. Those who are preparing for the Seniors Games have contact with a social group that spends more time with people at the local community recreation centre than with those at the bridge club. Thus the social milieu of the athletes is different from that of the card players even though both live in the same community and are of similar ages.

Findings from a study of retirement satisfaction of rural residents in Iowa (Dorfman et al., 1988) suggest that a marriage partner may be an important aspect of the social milieu. The authors found that the number of leisure activities engaged in with a spouse was positively associated with retirement satisfaction. The never married and widowed must develop their social environment from among friends and other kin.

A social milieu comprised of others in the same age group is sometimes seen as preferable because the group offers peer support. Findings of a study by Strain (1979) of seniors in two rural Manitoba communities suggest that this may not be the case for rural seniors. Strain found that the majority (67 percent) of respondents favoured age-integrated activities. Unfortunately programs for seniors, are often only offered through seniors' centres which have few such activities.

In rural communities, networks of family and friends may provide a different social milieu than they do in urban areas, thus affecting leisure patterns. Scott and Roberto (1987) found that patterns of involvement varied depending upon the activity. They found that rural elders aged 65 to 90 were less likely to engage in formal recreational pursuits such as going to concerts or movies, with children or with friends than were urban elders. However, rural residents were more likely to be involved with children in informal recreation such as outdoor activities, vacations and reunions. Scott and Roberto suggest that friends of rural elders are more likely than are friends of urban elders to serve practical, supportive functions such as helping with shopping, and giving support when ill.

Results of the General Recreation Survey conducted in Alberta (Alberta Recreation and Parks, 1988), suggest that rural residents have a more available social network with whom to engage in recreational activities than do urban residents. Among reasons for non-participation in recreational activities, 35 percent of people in cities of populations over 100,000 said they had no others with whom to participate. In towns of under 2000 residents, this was not among the top five reasons. Rather, distance and lack of access to recreational opportunities were the primary reasons for non-participation among rural residents.

Ethnic differences are another aspect of social milieu that may affect leisure participation. Ouellette (1986) investigated the effects of social class and ethnicity on the leisure activities and enjoyment of leisure of New Brunswick seniors. The sample for the study included three executive members and five non-board members for each of the 229 senior citizen clubs affiliated with the New Brunswick Senior Citizens' Federation. The total sample was 1832 people, of whom 62 percent were rural.

Ouellette postulated that among English and French speaking elders, ethnicity would influence involvement in types of social organizations. He also argued that within ethnic groups, social class and geographic location would cause people to act differently. Interestingly, he found that geographic location was not an indicator of leisure involvement or enjoyment. Age, social class and other demographic variables were more important. Those who were younger, had a higher social status, and had a more positive perception of their health, were more involved in leisure activities. Ethnicity affected types of leisure involvement, with English people less likely than French people to participate in religious activities including attending church.

Receptiveness

The final condition of adopting an activity according to the Brandenburg model, is receptiveness or willingness to enter into a new experience. A change in level of receptiveness may be generated by such things as life-cycle changes, change in domicile, or change of employment, all of which may occur in the life of a recently retired person. A long-standing desire to do something may be the basis of this receptiveness. For example, retirement may provide an individual who was previously constrained by time, social milieu and lack of opportunity to develop golfing skills with the opportunity to take up golfing.

In an ethnographic study of creative activities newly adopted by a group of ten Newfoundland men and women, Doucette (1987) suggests that receptiveness rather than social milieu may account for the taking up of a new art or craft activity by seniors. Doucette's thesis is that we need to better understand the meaning that creative work holds for aged individuals. The ten people in the study ranged in age from 54 to 84. They held in common a perception that they had entered a distinct life phase marked by retirement, completion of childrearing, widowhood or relocation. All saw the shift as having deep personal significance and requiring new approaches to life. Doucette sees the adoption of new activities as one strategy used to adjust to these changes.

We know relatively little about the interaction of the factors that Brandenburg et al. suggest are instrumental in the adoption of leisure. Nor do we know how the importance of these factors might vary within rural communities and within age cohorts of seniors. Although further exploration of these questions is warranted, the goals of that exploration must be made explicit. Surely a fundamental question asked by leisure programmers must be whether potential participants are interested in taking on new activities. Mobily et al. (1987) surveyed 3097 rural midwestern seniors aged 65 and over. When respondents were asked about physical activity, most felt that their daily chores gave them enough exercise and approximately 40 percent felt that they did not need to get more exercise. According to the authors, this response indicates that most respondents failed to recognize that daily chores did not give them enough exercise. Another possible conclusion is that the researchers failed to assess the leisure attitudes of the respondents in their study. In an effort to reduce ageism, it is possible to impose unreasonable expectations of standards of excellence.

Descriptions of the activities of rural seniors and of the two cases from Chapter 1 show that there are real gaps in our understanding of life-long patterns of activity, in motivation to take part in leisure and in variations in leisure patterns. Because we have not investigated attitudes toward work of most rural seniors, it is not possible to determine how many retirees have leisure activities that spill over from previous work.

Those who have lived and worked in closely knit remote communities may engage in leisure activities that are similar to work because opportunities for compensatory activities are limited. They may also have little leisure if they are still involved in work or see barriers to leisure involvement.

Since they have moved to Kaslo from Vancouver, Ruth and Al Wilson have removed themselves from leisure activities that require urban facilities. Before they came to Kaslo, they played squash and swam at a fitness club that was close to work. One of their reasons for moving to Kaslo was to develop a lifestyle in which physical activity was built into daily life. In the short time they have been in Kaslo, they have planted a large garden, bought bicycles to cycle into town and learned to split wood for the fireplace. They feel that they are in better shape and are under less stress than they have been for years. The Wilsons would likely disagree with Mobily et al. who suggest that daily chores do not provide seniors with enough physical exercise. Because the Wilsons chose to move to a new community, they are receptive to new activities. And because of their education and experience, they are likely to have or develop knowledge of leisure activities in their new community.

Since Murray Nelson is a long-time resident of Kaslo, he has the advantage of a cohort of friends with whom to participate in leisure activities. However, he is less likely to develop new activities since there is more continuity in his life than there is for the Wilsons. Murray Nelson now gets less physical exercise than ever before since he is doing very little farming. However, he sees no need to be more active and sees more sedentary activities, such as fishing, as a reward for a lifetime of hard physical labour.

SUMMARY AND CONCLUSIONS

This chapter was begun with the assumption that among rural seniors, work was highly valued but that leisure was not part of the rural ethic. Statistics on workforce involvement of rural seniors show that many farmers over age 65 continue to work. However, self-employed workers such as farmers are just as likely to be working because of financial need as because of a love for farming. It is time to get rid of the stereotype of the idyllic farm life according to which people enjoy working into old age. There are several barriers to employment for rural seniors including large distances to employment opportunities, sanctions against the employment of women and chronic job shortages in some rural areas. Nonetheless the types of jobs done by non-farm rural residents are no different in scope from those of urban dwellers.

Little is known about retirement of rural workers other than farmers. We do not know whether retirement from a job such as teaching is different for rural than for urban dwellers. We need to better understand the significance of retirement for rural workers, and the factors that might influence post-retirement adjustment. An important avenue for further investigation is the impact on rural communities of urban dwellers (such as Ruth and Al Wilson) who move to rural areas after retirement. Their experiences, expectations about services and level of income may be quite different from those of long-time rural residents and may have a profound impact on small communities that become retirement centres.

Research on the leisure activities and patterns of rural dwellers does not indicate that rural seniors avoid leisure activities. Rather, their patterns of activity are different from those of urban residents. Rural seniors tend to engage in more land-based than facility-based activities; to be involved in more age-integrated activities; to be involved in leisure with family members and to have a social group with whom to take part in activities. For those who retire and stay in the same community, there may be less impetus to take on new activities than for those who move to a new community. We need to begin to look without an urban bias at leisure needs of seniors, and to better understand opportunities for leisure in a variety of rural settings such as single resource areas and those that are remote from service centres. Practitioners and researchers also need to ask themselves whether the level of activity of rural seniors is adequate. It is futile to attempt to raise activity levels among those who feel that the level of activity in their daily lives as already adequate.

CHAPTER 3

INDEPENDENT LIVING

"The fundamental principle in the care of the elderly should be to enable them to lead independent lives in their communities for as long as possible" (National Advisory Council on Aging, 1983: 84). This statement illustrates both the high value placed on independence of the elderly and the belief that part of the operational definition of independence is the ability to live within the community. The goal of independent living appears to guide much of the research and policy regarding rural elders and it is one of the basic tenets of the rural ideology discussed in Chapter 1. However, there are few conceptual or operational definitions of independence. Thus, it is difficult to assess level of independence of rural elders, to compare their levels of independence to those of urban elders, or to determine what interventions are necessary to improve or maintain independence. The purpose of this chapter is to develop a definition of independent living, to review studies that assess levels of independence of rural elders and to discuss issues affecting and approaches to increasing that degree of independence.

A DEFINITION OF INDEPENDENCE

Although there are few explicit definitions of independence, three major criteria are implicit in the research on the independence of seniors. The first criterion is the ability of individuals to maintain control over their near environment; their ability to meet personal basic needs (Alberta Senior Citizens' Secretariat, 1986) and to maintain responsibility for decisions in these areas (McClelland and Miles, 1987). The concept of 'dignity of risk' is an aspect of this definition of independence and includes the idea that even those with physical and mental disabilities should be able to make their own decisions and should be allowed to risk making mistakes (Ontario Advisory Council for Disabled Persons, 1988). Operational definitions of control include the ability to carry out activities of daily living, and the ability to live in a physical setting that has sufficient facilities to allow for ease of managing these tasks.

The second criterion is that the individual is a part of the community. Narrowly defined, this means living in the community rather than living in an institutional setting. More broadly, it has come to mean the fullest possible integration into the community (Ontario Advisory Council for Disabled Persons, 1988). Community integration includes maintaining a separate household (as opposed to living with children) (Kivett and Learner, 1980); not being homebound (Fritz and Orlowski, 1983); and not living in an institutional setting (Neufeldt, 1974). Other aspects that determine community integration are involvement in leisure and work activities (discussed in Chapter 2), and having adequate physical and mental health to participate in the community (discussed in Chapter 4).

The third criterion of independent living is ease of access to services. The assumption here is that a person cannot remain in the community if he or she does not have access to basic services such as groceries, pharmacies, health care, banking, etc. The need for services to be accessible has been seen as the greatest need of seniors (Havens, 1980). There is controversy over which factor best measures access; is it distance or some other factor such as cultural barriers or cost? The great emphasis by researchers on the evaluation of transportation difficulties suggests that distance is seen by social scientists and planners as a major barrier to access.

Although the concept of independent living may also have other meanings, for the purposes of this chapter it will be defined to include the three elements described above: control over the near environment, integration into the community and access to services. Operational definitions will be discussed under each of these headings.

Independence and the Rural Elderly

Research and policy on the rural elderly appears to have been guided by two sets of assumptions about independence. The first assumption is that, because of the environment in which they live, it is more difficult for rural than urban elders to maintain their independence. The rural elderly have been seen as facing the "double jeopardy" of old age and a difficult living situation. Using the traditional indicators of health, income and housing, elders in rural areas are seen as having a poorer quality of life than that enjoyed by urban elders (Krout, 1988). The second assumption is that despite the difficult environment, or perhaps because of it, rural elders place high value on independence and have personality traits and methods of maintaining independence that are different from those in urban areas.

The 'independent rural personality' is the topic of much folklore in the literature on rural elders. The following statement is typical: "Rural seniors have typically spent a lifetime looking after themselves and they do not seem to be interested in the idea that anyone else might do more for them" (Ontario Advisory Council on Senior Citizens, 1980: 15). Those living in the north and native seniors are examples of two groups of rural elders seen by rural professionals as being strongly independent.

The North's seniors are the homesteaders who opened the land. In many cases these individuals are suspicious of government. They are not familiar with bureaucratic red tape. When a job is to be done, they believe nothing should stop it from being achieved (Peace River Health Unit, 1986: 54).

"Older natives are very proud and independent. Their resistance to going outside the reserve, settlement or community is very great" (Hohn, 1986: 21). Policy makers certainly seem to believe that independence is part of the rural ideology.

McNeil et al. (1986) provide one promising direction for moving from folklore to systematic examination of the 'independent rural personality'. They have developed a measure of psychological hardiness in adults over age 60. Their construct of hardiness has three components: commitment, control and challenge.

Commitment is a tendency to be involved in ongoing activity, rather than to feel indifferent to it or lack purpose. Control is a belief in personal power to influence the course of life events, rather than helplessness in the face of external forces. Challenge is a perception of change as usual in life and a stimulus to growth, rather than as a threat to security (1986: 43).

One might expect that if the stereotypical rural personality does exist, rural elders would score high on psychological hardiness. There has been no research on rural seniors which addresses this question.

Based on these assumptions of an apparent contradiction between an environment in which it is difficult for seniors to maintain independence and a personality or value stance that requires independence, research on elements of independence of rural elders is reviewed in the following sections.

CONTROL OVER THE NEAR ENVIRONMENT

Housing Conditions and Facilities

The elderly from the farm and countryside evidently retire to hamlets, villages and small towns, elderly small towners tend to stay there and there is also the movement of some elderly persons from cities to retire in small communities. But beyond the broad tendencies and preliminary projections, we know very little about the living environments of the elderly in small communities (Hodge, 1984: 2).

Many studies have compared housing of rural and urban elders. When this comparison is made, rural elders are seen to be badly served. By all objective measures, rural elders have fewer amenities in their near environments than do their urban counterparts.

Table 3.1 shows the ages of houses of urban, rural-farm and rural non-farm residents of all ages. Regional differences in the age of housing reflect the settlement patterns in the country with people in the west living in newer houses. Urban housing tends to be newer than rural housing. More urban than rural dwellers live in housing built since 1971, while more

TABLE 3.1

PERIOD OF CONSTRUCTION OF PRIVATE DWELLINGS, FOR CANADA AND PROVINCES URBAN, RURAL NON-FARM, RURAL FARM, 1981

Location	Total Dwellings	Percentage of Homes by Period of Construction			
		pre 1921	1921-45	1946-70	1971-81
Canada					
Urban	6,508,685	9	13	47	31
Rural non-farm	1,500,390	15	12	34	40
Rural farm	272,450	32	16	30	22
Newfoundland					
Urban	90,065	8	12	47	33
Rural non-farm	57,905	9	13	42	35
Rural farm	445	6	20	46	29
Prince Edward Island					
Urban	14,930	20	15	36	29
Rural non-farm	19,755	27	12	23	39
Rural farm	2,975	55	13	17	15
Nova Scotia					
Urban	156,805	19	16	37	28
Rural non-farm	111,815	25	11	30	34
Rural farm	4,570	59	10	16	14
New Brunswick					
Urban	116,595	16	15	40	29
Rural non-farm	94,560	18	13	28	42
Rural farm	3,765	53	11	19	17
Quebec					
Urban	1,751,750	9	14	50	27
Rural non-farm	378,115	17	12	30	41
Rural farm	42,990	48	17	19	16
Ontario					
Urban	2,482,865	10	13	47	28
Rural non-farm	411,915	20	10	37	33
Rural farm	75,005	58	11	17	14
Manitoba					
Urban	270,000	10	15	47	29
Rural non-farm	63,205	10	15	39	36
Rural farm	24,780	17	19	41	23
Saskatchewan					
Urban	205,430	7	13	47	34
Rural non-farm	76,665	12	19	37	32
Rural farm	50,615	16	21	40	23
Alberta					
Urban	608,475	3	6	43	48
Rural non-farm	98,940	6	14	32	48
Rural farm	50,825	8	18	42	32
British Columbia					
Urban	800,015	5	12	46	37
Rural non-farm	180,145	3	8	36	53
Rural farm	16,480	7	15	40	38

SOURCE: Statistics Canada (1984b) *Occupied Private Dwellings, 1981 Census of Canada.* Table 7, Catalogue # 92-932.

farmers live in houses built before 1921. Farm elders (51 percent) are much more likely than non-farm (38 percent) or urban (30 percent) elders to live in houses built before 1920 (Stone and Fletcher, 1980).

Among rural residents, farmers live in older housing. However, there are substantial regional differences within the farm group. Approximately half of eastern farmers, from Prince Edward Island to Ontario, live in houses built before 1921, while western farmers are much more likely to live in new housing. This difference presumably reflects the more recent settlement of the west, although it may also reflect a lack of sentiment for older buildings in the west. In Canada, eastern farmers appear to have the oldest houses in the worst state of repair, indications of the economic status of farming in that region.

The relative deprivation of the near environment of rural elders can also be measured in terms of the adequacy of housing facilities. Chamberlain (1976) has argued that certain facilities are necessary for a person to be adequately housed. These are: hot and cold running water inside the house, indoor toilet, indoor bath or shower, central heat, electricity, gas or electric stove and refrigerator. In a study of rural elders in North Frontenac, a county in central Ontario, Chamberlain described some of the housing disadvantages of rural elders. Only half of the seniors in North Frontenac had central heating as compared to 90 percent of seniors in the province. North Frontenac seniors were also less likely than Ontario seniors in general to have hot and cold running water (65 percent versus 96 percent), bath or shower (63 percent versus 97 percent), or indoor toilet (73 percent versus 97 percent). Most people who were without one facility were lacking in several. Among those without hot and cold running water, most were without central heat, lived in houses of less than 1,000 square feet and cooked with a wood stove.

People in remote areas and those on reserves may be even less well served. Hohn (1986) states that in 1977 fewer than 40 percent of the houses on rural and remote reserves had running water, sewage disposal and indoor plumbing compared to 60 percent in all Canadian rural homes. A more recent survey in 1983 showed that 75 percent of elders on the Frog Lake Reserve in Alberta had no indoor plumbing and 92 percent were without telephones.

Not only are rural elders living in older houses with fewer facilities, they are also likely to be concerned about high costs of home maintenance. In a survey of seniors in 65 municipalities in Nova Scotia, the Senior Citizens Research Committee (1980) found that 40 percent of respondents experienced difficulty in meeting their tax payments. Of those who had sold their homes, the major reasons given were high cost, difficulty of home maintenance and the high cost of property taxes. Results of a study of rural elders conducted in Ontario were similar. Fritz and Orlowski (1983) found that housing was the most pressing consumer concern. High taxes, rising costs of rent and other financial considerations were the most serious housing concerns.

Some researchers have suggested that there is a direct link between quality of housing and an ability to meet basic needs, one of the criteria for independent living. The Alberta Senior Citizens' Secretariat (1986: 12) states that

> "housing . . . potentially affects all areas of one's life. If one's residence is not clean and in good repair, it can become a hazard to physical health. If it is confining, unappealing and not satisfactory to the person, it can negatively affect mental health and social life. If it is isolating and lacks accessibility to services and transportation, it can handicap a person socially and affect physical well-being".

Others agree that there is a link between physical and social problems and quality of housing. "Poor housing has a positive correlation with poor health" (Fiaz, 1983: 18). Findings from a comparison of native and non-native rural elders in Manitoba support this argument. Bienvenue and Havens (1986) found that greater proportions of native than non-native elders reported that their bathroom and kitchen facilities were inadequate and that they had insufficient heat, light and privacy. The authors suggest that these poor housing conditions pose health risks since lack of heat and sanitation are related to the occurrence of communicable diseases.

Similar links are proposed between quality of housing and general well being. Michalos (1982) conducted a study of the life satisfaction of 392 rural elders in Huron County, Ontario. Average age was 77 and approximately half (46 percent) were farmers. Michalos found that differences in housing, health and self-esteem accounted for 49 percent of the variation in life-satisfaction. The most important element of life-satisfaction was satisfaction with housing. Michalos notes that interventions to improve life-satisfaction could include help with home repair or a lowering of property taxes.

Although much of the research on housing suggests that poor housing resources influence health or life satisfaction, findings from research by Windley and Scheidt (1988) indicate that the relationship may be more complex. The authors studied the perceptions of their environments held by small town elders in Kansas. They categorized respondents under four headings from frail to fully engaged, based on measures of mental and physical health, contact with others, and level of participation in activities. Elders who were considered frail were significantly more likely to be dissatisfied with all aspects of their homes. The authors suggest that this dissatisfaction may be due to their increased vulnerability to environmental factors such as, for example, slippery sidewalks in winter. They did not suggest that differences were due to the fact that frail elders lived in poorer quality housing than others. Rather than being a direct reflection of adequacy of housing, housing disatisfaction may be a proxy for vulnerability to the near environment.

Objective findings on housing and housing facilities support the contention that rural elders often have inadequate housing. Yet, these findings tell us little about the relationship between quality of housing and perceived adequacy of that housing. One fruitful area of investigation might be an exploration of which objective aspects of housing are critical in influencing the ability of residents to maintain control of their near environments. It seems unlikely that age of housing is an important indicator. The retired Ontario farm couple who have carefully restored great-grandfather's stone farmhouse would surely consider themselves greatly advantaged in terms of their housing environment. However, some housing facilities may be especially important for some groups of elders. For example, in the Northwest Territories and the Yukon, housing must be constructed above the ground to avoid melting the permafrost subsurface and to accommodate contours of the land. Hence, most buildings have several steps, making it difficult for those with disabilities to get in and out easily (McClelland and Miles, 1987). Ease of access could make the difference in the ability of a disabled older person to continue to live at home. Another example of the difference between quality of housing and perceived adequacy of housing is the tradition among some native families to maintain three- and four-generation households. Such traditions are not easily accommodated within the contemporary Canadian approach to new housing, which is to build small houses for three- or four-person families. Some flexibility in design of new housing could facilitate rather than hinder traditional approaches to inter-generational living. Creative solutions to such special housing problems as these are essential if people are to remain in their own homes.

Further exploration of indirect relationships between housing facilities, health and life-satisfaction may be useful in determining how both objective and perceived levels of resources in the near environment can affect the ability to have control over that environment. Perceived adequacy of housing may be more important to independence than any objective measure. The urban resident who retires to the countryside may find heating with wood is more than she can manage, if she cannot afford to buy the wood and have it stacked near her door. A long-time resident of the area may cut the wood herself or have friends who will do that for her.

The Personal Environment

One aspect of control over the near environment is an ability to care for personal needs, often subsumed under the category of activities of daily living (ADLs). Such activities include bathing, dressing, eating, and walking. There have been few studies of the ability of rural elders to perform activities of daily living, or comparisons between the effects of the rural versus the urban environment on the ability of elders to manage daily tasks.

One of the few studies to directly address this question was conducted by Coward and Cutler (1988). Using data from the United States National Health Interview Survey, they compared differences in the degree to which activities of daily living are performed with difficulty by elders living in four residential situations. Four residential categories were used: central city, not central city, farm, non-farm. All respondents were over age 65. Of seven ADLs (dressing, bathing, eating, getting in and out of bed or chairs, walking, getting outside, using the toilet), there were significant differences in the ability of elders belonging to the various residential categories to walk and get outside. There were also significant differences in the numbers of ADLs performed with difficulty. Residents of rural non-farm areas had the most difficulty in performing tasks; farm residents the least. The authors suggest that these differences may be a function of the fact that farms are only classified as farms if they earn an income over $1000. Thus, there may have been a bias toward healthy elders who were still farming. Older farmers may also be more physically fit because of their active lifestyle. There is a need for systematic evaluation of variations in the ability of rural elders to perform ADLs.

As with other aspects of independence, attitudes of elders toward ADLs may be as important as actual abilities. Raiwet (1989) conducted extensive interviews with couples living in remote areas of the Peace River district of Alberta. She was interested in how these couples coped with the physical changes that accompany age. Many had chronic illnesses that were quite disabling by objective standards. One man had arthritis so badly that he could not turn his head, but he continued to split his own wood using a splitter that he had invented to compensate for his physical problems. Raiwet found that independence for these people was a matter of doing what they wanted to do. Most compensated for activities they could not do by increased use of technology, by relying on their spouse or other family members or by changing their activities. One woman rarely left the house but counted on others to visit her at home.

Although we now have adequate assessment tools to measure the functional status of older people, we know much less about what Rowles (1988) has called the phenomenological perspective of rural elders. Rowles argues that in order to understand aging, we need to know about the ways in which individuals organize and create their worlds as well as about their objective circumstances. Control over the personal environment may be influenced as much by how people view their physical abilities as by their objective functional status.

INTEGRATION INTO THE COMMUNITY

The Wish to Remain at Home

Assumptions about community integration are seen primarily in the assertion that rural elders, like their urban counterparts, wish to remain in their own homes in their own communities. Studies in all parts of the country, in both rural and urban areas, confirm that this is the first choice in accommodation. Typical are findings from an evaluation of the housing preferences of 311 elders in Moose Jaw, Saskatchewan. Sixty six percent preferred to remain in their own homes and fully 97 percent wished to be close to their old neighbourhood, family and friends (Agbayewa and Michalski, 1984).

In a study of rural elders in Alberta, Keating and Brundin (1983) found that remaining at home was the first choice of rural retirees. However, those who had recently retired faced two different housing choices. The first, shortly after retirement, was the possibility of moving to a new house on the farm or to a house in the nearest community. This decision was seen positively and was prompted by the desire to have a new house, the wish to let farming children live in the farm house or the convenience of a smaller dwelling. The second decision, made at a later time, was seen as one that would be imposed by circumstances such as poor health or widowhood. That move was anticipated as an imposed choice that was required because of increased dependence. Most hoped that they would not have to make that move.

In general, rural seniors choose to remain in their own homes even when they need more supportive care. In a survey of the need for support services of seniors in Kent County, Ontario (Kent County District Health Council, 1983), the group of people who were being least well-served were those who were living in their own homes but who needed acute or extended care. The major reason that they were not receiving this care was their wish to remain in their own homes as long as possible. This is one of the major dilemmas of maintaining independence. Despite overwhelming evidence that elders prefer to remain at home, problems of service delivery in rural areas mitigate against meeting this need for some seniors.

Attachment to the Community

The wish to remain in the community is only one aspect of community involvement. A strong sense of being part of a supportive community and an attachment to that community, also contribute to independence. Kivett (1988a) describes two characteristics which are central, for elders to maintain a sense of community. The first is that communities are made up of friends and neighbours who serve as dependable, available resources. The second is that communities also allow for a sense of privacy. Thus, rural communities provide support when needed but also allow the elder to maintain a measure of personal control over the use of that support.

Attachment to community may be especially strong for those living in remote areas and for native seniors. One study which addresses this question examined the needs of seniors in the Peace River district of Alberta (Peace River Health Unit, 1986). The study included more than 400 seniors, many of them original settlers of the area. Respondents were divided into two groups, rural and "remote". "Remote" residents were primarily native seniors who lived in isolated areas. They had many of the characteristics of the bypassed remote rural area discussed in Chapter 1. Many did not speak English (40 percent) or read it (51 percent). They had an average of three years', formal education.

Strong community attachment is evident in the disinclination of these people to relocate, even for health reasons. While 59 percent of rural residents said they would move if their health required them to do so, only 28 percent of "remote" residents were willing to move under the same circumstances. "Remote" residents were more likely to live with their families and to expect their families to take care of them if necessary. Attachment to a community may also be rather passive, indicating a lack of alternatives. While half of the seniors in more settled areas had made some plans for their old age, only 10 percent of "remote" seniors had done so. The authors state that "it was clear that all respondents placed great value on their independence and would do whatever they could to remain as independent as possible for as long as possible" (Peace River Health Unit, 1986: 68).

Other authors have also suggested that native elders may be even more bound to their communities than are non-native seniors in remote areas. Positive reasons for such attachment may include strong ties to family and a tradition of living in multigeneration families. A study of the living situation of native elders on a reserve in northern Alberta (Hohn, 1986: 24) showed that 98 percent of those over 60 had grandchildren living with them. The consensus was "that this was of their own invite and that they wished to have their grandchildren living with them and had requested that their children allow them to do so". The author says that strong ties and responsibilities to family may mean that elders remain in their own homes long after they require more care. "Because of their great devotion to family harmony and dependency on family members, often older natives allow their own needs to come last" (Hohn, 1986: 27). High costs of fuel in northern areas and the deemed inhospitable nature of institutional settings, add to the resistance by native elders to going into an institution outside the reserve. And, the lack of native foods and language in nearby institutions means that such settings are seen by them as inadequate to provide the care that is necessary. Elders foresee visits from family members dwindling to none if they are institutionalized. For this group of seniors, there seems to be little ground between full integration into the community and isolation from it.

The situation of seniors in other remote communities is likely quite similar. If there is only one extended care facility it may be unable to meet various needs from independence to full-time care. Thus, "remote" seniors may only have access to services that assume greater dependency than actually exists.

A promising direction in understanding the issue of community involvement is that taken by Scheidt (1984) in a study of 1000 older residents of towns with populations ranging from 100 to 2,500. Scheidt was interested in the structure of well-being of these rural seniors. He measured several areas of satisfaction: for example, housing, neighbourhood, mobility, etc., as well as three criteria of well-being. A subsequent factor analysis showed four major patterns of integration into the community. The four types were: fully engaged (19 percent of sample), partially-engaged (46 percent), disengaged and frail. The majority of each group lived in their own homes and all but the frail elderly reported good mental and physical health. Thus, living independently in the community was not a factor that distinguished the groups. However, the groups were differentiated by their varying amounts of activity and involvement with others. The fully engaged group had frequent contact with friends and relatives and was involved in the greatest number of community activities. The partially-engaged group had fewer home visits with friends and relatives but was engaged in several town activities. The disengaged group had little social or community involvement and cited many social and physical barriers to community involvement. Finally, the frail group had poorer physical and mental health, with little social contact or community activity. The latter two groups had similar levels of involvement, but for different reasons. For the disengaged, lack of involvement was primarily for social reasons. For the frail, reasons for isolation tended to be physical. These findings suggest that community involvement is a more sensitive indicator of independence than is community living.

Development of a New Community

One way to increase the chances of maintaining independence is to have long-standing community relationships. Another is to move into a purpose-built community that is designed with amenities to enhance quality of life and independence. Just beginning to appear in the Canadian research literature is information on communities developed especially for retirees. Retirement communities are groups of housing units planned for healthy, older people who are retired, physically active and well (Hunt et al., 1984; Ontario Ministry of Municipal Affairs, 1985). These communities have emerged because of a higher standard of living, greater personal savings and expanded retirement benefits which have helped produce a generation of middle class retirees (Break, 1985). Developments normally incorporate shared facilities and services, especially recreational facilities. The provision of services helps create a community from what would otherwise be merely a collection of housing units (Hunt et al., 1984).

A large proportion of retirement communities are located in rural and recreational areas (Ontario Ministry of Municipal Affairs, 1985). Many are outside existing communities, sometimes in isolated areas. Those built in rural areas are designed to meet the needs of relatively young, affluent, retirees. One aspect of these communities that has not been investigated is how well they meet the changing needs of residents as they age. Healthy, active, independent seniors in their 60s may be well-served by an isolated rural community with good recreational facilities and a new group of congenial neighbours. The same group of seniors may find, in their 80s, that their community cannot meet their changing needs.

Barriers to Remaining in the Community

Findings described in the monograph on victimization and fear of crime among the elderly (Brillon, 1987) indicate that a safe environment is important to Canada's elders. Brillon reports that seniors are more likely than other age groups to think that crime rates in Canada have increased. However, when asked whether crime had increased in their neighbourhoods, Canadians of all ages perceived similar rates of increase. Brillon concludes that crime is seen as a problem by seniors on a relatively abstract level.

In comparison to urban elders, rural elders generally have fewer problems with crime. Brillon (1987: 38) reports that the risk of becoming a victim is five times higher in urban than rural areas.

> It would seem, then, that life in a rural area is quieter, that there is less opportunity for crime (fewer things to steal, not so many bars, etc.) and that there is stricter control of the community. Families know their neighbours and are more or less aware of everyone's comings and goings. The people lack the anonymity of the large city with its possibility of getting lost in the crowd and avoiding surveillance of any kind. The daily life and way of thinking could explain the big difference between the two environments.

Similar findings come from The Ontario Advisory Council on Senior Citizens (1980). They compared rural and urban seniors and found that rural seniors felt less threatened by crime. In a more detailed analysis of the personal safety concerns of rural and urban elders in Newfoundland and Labrador, Vivian (1982) studied a representative sample of seniors from all parts of the province. She found that 11 percent of respondents living in communities with populations of 2,000 or greater, compared to 7 percent of those living in smaller communities reported worrying about personal safety. Safety concerns in order of most to least mentioned were theft or vandalism, winter walking and driving, fire, being alone at night, and dangerous walking conditions. There were no differences in between those in larger and smaller communities in the way they ranked these concerns. Only a small proportion of concerns were related to crime. More important were concerns about environmental hazards that might impede walking or driving. These low reported rates of concern about crime or personal safety may reflect the fact that rural seniors see themselves living in a benign environment. It may also mean that rural seniors do exemplify the stereotype of being hardy and independent and have learned to deal with being alone or with winter hazards. This is an issue worthy of further examination in a country in which climatic conditions are less than benign and where independent seniors might not ask for needed assistance.

ACCESS TO SERVICES

In Chapter 1 part of the discussion of what is meant by "rural" was centred on distance from services. This issue has been of great concern to practitioners and policy makers because the ability to gain access to services is seen as a critical element in the ability to live independently. In one of the most comprehensive studies of access to services, Hodge (1984) developed a list of basic community resources and applied to these the two indices of availability and accessibility. This list includes 12 resources which he says are essential to seniors in their communities: bank, grocery store, doctor, church, post office, drug store, beauty shop/barber, restaurant, social club, variety store, department store, clothing store/shoe store. These basic community resources were identified by seniors in a study in several small communities in eastern Ontario. The resources were those used most often by seniors in those communities. Each was used by at least 25 percent of respondents.

Hodge (1984: 56) says that these services are used extensively by seniors in small communities if they are available and accessible. He defines availability as "both the extent to which each of the basic resources is present and the degree of choice that exists". His operational definition, which he calls the "index of availability", is a ratio of the total number of establishments offering the basic resource divided by the number of basic resources present. The higher the index, the greater the availability. Accessibility is the average walking distance to basic resources. The latter definition is justified, based on the fact that in the small communities he studied, people liked to walk and did walk to most activities. Clearly, accessibility is a different issue for farming communities and those remote rural communities with few of the basic services identified by Hodge.

Of the nine towns studied, Hodge found that those with populations over 2,000 had higher availability indices than towns of under 1,000. Hodge concludes that optimal levels of availability are likely to occur in towns with populations over 2,000. In terms of accessibility, Hodge found that 500 metres was a preferred upper limit for average walking distance to community resources. Hodge concludes that a positive resource environment requires both availability and accessibility of resources.

An interesting contrast to the objective indices of availability and accessibility of services developed by Hodge, is found in the work by Windley and Scheidt (1988) on what they call the perceptual environment of rural elders. They examined how 898 elderly residents of small towns of different sizes (100 to 500, 501 to 1500 and 1501 to 2500) perceived twelve aspects of their rural environments. All of the towns were in Kansas. The authors found no differences in awareness of services or in perceived access to services among residents in towns of different sizes. However, differences emerged when residents were divided into four groups based on health (mental and physical), contact with others, and activity participation. The frail group scored lowest on all three factors; the fully engaged highest on all three.

Windley and Scheidt found that the frail group was relatively well-informed about the existence of services in their communities and used those services more than did some other groups. However, they reported significantly greater numbers of barriers to access to community services. "They complained to a greater extent about the lack of adequate street lighting, walking distance, lack of available rides, hazardous routes and busy streets" (1988: 157). Since the frail group was living in the same communities as the other groups, these complaints were not based on objective assessments of community resources. Rather, the negative evaluation of the environment was based more on personality and personal attributes such as an ability to walk comfortably, than on the availability of services.

Findings from this study and those of Hodge suggest that both the objective and perceptual environments need to be evaluated in order to determine whether a community has adequate services. Windley and Scheidt also suggest that programs and services may need to be targeted to specific communities since one kind of intervention may not be appropriate in all communities. Concepts of what is a comfortable distance to services may be different for in-migrants from cities with high density services than for farmers who are used to driving long distances for basic needs such as groceries.

Access Through Transportation

The majority of the research on accessibility is based on the assumption that most rural seniors do not live in a positive resource environment since many services they require are at a distance. Transportation is the means by which most rural seniors gain access to needed services. In general, rural seniors are transportation disadvantaged because of the lack of public transportation and their dependence on private cars.

One of the most comprehensive studies of transportation for the elderly was conducted in Saskatchewan in 1981 and 1985. The first part of the study involved 1675 rural seniors from three "relatively remote" regions of the province; the second was a comparative sample of 1275 urban seniors (Senior Citizens Provincial Council, 1987). Samples were similar in age, with a mean age of approximately 73.

Since the study dealt with transportation difficulties, it was oriented toward describing existing problems. Respondents were all asked to "rank the degree of transportation difficulty that they usually experience in pursuing their daily activities (Senior Citizens Provincial Council, 1987: 19). Twenty-one percent of the rural sample and 15 percent of the urban seniors stated that they had a transportation problem.

When those with serious transportation problems were ranked by size of community, the least disadvantaged were those on farms (9 percent). The most disadvantaged were those in towns of 1000 to 5000 people (20 percent) and those in towns with less than 1000 people (23 percent). The lack of transportation problems cited by farm residents, despite greater distances to services, paradoxically reflects the great potential for severe transportation problems among farm elders. Those who remain on the farm usually have their own cars. Those who cannot drive may be forced to move into the nearest town since access is virtually impossible without a car.

For both urban and rural residents, the easiest destination was the home of a best friend; the most distant and therefore difficult destinations were the homes of family members and the physician. With the exception of those on farms who walked to very few destinations, seniors in communities of less than 5000 were more likely to walk to all destinations than those in urban areas.

Approximately half of both rural and urban seniors drove themselves to destinations. The next most common mode of transportation was to ride with someone else. Although rural seniors lived further from their friends, relatives and children and transportation to those destinations was problematic, the frequency of social interaction for urban and rural seniors was virtually identical (Senior Citizens Provincial Council, 1987). Thus, although the report indicated that rural residents lack local bus service and must travel longer distances to frequent destinations, they apparently managed a level of interaction similar to their urban counterparts.

In contrast to the Saskatchewan study, seniors in Newfoundland and Labrador report virtually no transportation problems (Vivian, 1982). Ninety-seven percent of respondents said they were satisfied with the customary means of transportation. The sample was representative of urban and rural areas of all parts of the province. Despite this high level of satisfaction, most did not own or drive a car. Of those aged 65 to 74, only 26 percent owned a car, while 20 percent drove a car. Most said that they walked or were driven to destinations by family. Those in small communities of 100 to 2000 residents had the most transportation problems, but only 4 percent of these residents said that help with transportation would be welcome. Differences in these findings may be regional or they may reflect the fact that the Saskatchewan study was problem oriented.

Seniors appear willing to forgo many conveniences to maintain independence. In a survey of consumer concerns of seniors in Guelph, Ontario, transportation was second after housing on the list of consumer concerns (Fritz and Orlowski, 1983). The cost of fuel, cars and taxis was part of the concern, as was the need for more public transportation. However, many people felt that although they would like more accessible transportation, they could do without it. Other studies present more negative analyses of the transportation difficulties of rural seniors. A report from the Ontario Advisory Council on Senior Citizens (1980) says that rural seniors are less satisfied than are urban seniors with transportation and are disadvantaged because of their absolute reliance on private cars.

Joseph and Fuller (1988: 32) speculate that there may have been too much emphasis placed on transportation "as a separate function in rural life". Their argument is that transportation is not important of itself but because of the services to which it provides access. Since there has been no assessment of the relationship between transportation dependence and service need, it is difficult to know whether transportation is a good indicator of independence for rural seniors.

SUMMARY AND CONCLUSIONS

Our knowledge of issues related to the independence of rural elders is very uneven. The finding that seniors wish to remain in their own homes has been substantiated and appears to require no further investigation. Remaining at home appears to be one of the important symbols of independence. Yet since most seniors do remain in their own homes, there is little variation in this element of independence. If the major definition of independence was community dwelling, it would be reasonable to conclude that the vast majority of rural seniors are independent and that we need have little concern for this issue.

In contrast, findings of the relatively poor quality of housing for rural seniors would suggest that many are at risk of not having a good-quality near environment. We have yet to determine which aspects of the physical environment might enhance their sense of control over the home environment. Further exploration will help identify subgroups of rural seniors who feel most disadvantaged by the lack of urban amenities.

It would be useful for rural practitioners to stop emphasizing better access to transportation as a primary solution to problems of maintaining independence. Developing creative approaches to the provision of transportation in rural areas may be admirable. However, it begs the question of what needs will be met by transportation. Until we have better data on unmet needs from the perspective of rural elders, it seems premature to develop services to meet those needs.

A systematic mapping of community resources combined with the collection of information on the availability of services, as perceived by rural elders, could be very useful both to town planners and to those service professionals who would try to be of assistance to rural seniors. We need to remind ourselves that the very help that is intended to increase independence may foster dependence. For example, a transportation service might be developed in the small town of Kaslo, B.C., described in Chapter 1. For Murray Nelson who has lived in the community all his life, it may be preferable to have a van pick him up and take him to work rather than have to drive his old car in winter on icy roads. However, in the absence of that service he will probably continue to drive to work or use his community contacts for car pools or lifts when necessary. We need to consider carefully the impact on seniors of the services we develop.

Finally, it seems that we must pay more attention to the ways in which seniors define independence and the strategies they use to maintain that independence. Here too, there are likely to be great variations among subgroups of rural seniors. While elderly farmers may remain in control by withholding transfer of the farm, native elders may do so by providing accommodation in their homes to extended family members. We need to focus more on how seniors themselves define independence, in order to understand how their strategies make sense to them.

CHAPTER 4

FAMILY AND SOCIAL NETWORKS

A fundamental belief about rural Canada is that rural elders are embedded in extended, supportive families, whose members are connected to one another through work and a common feeling of closeness to the land. Rural families are presumed to be close knit and private and to 'take care of their own', including their elders (Cape, 1984). The purpose of this chapter is to address some of these assumptions through an examination of the structure and interaction of older rural families.

HOUSEHOLD STRUCTURE OF RURAL SENIORS

As discussed in Chapter 1, the history of rural families in Canada lies in farming. Especially in the early days, when farming was often a subsistence operation, a large, unpaid family labour-force was necessary to run such a labour-intensive family business (Arcury, 1984). In contrast, the ideal urban family had few dependents since its livelihood was dependent on the wages of the primary breadwinner. Unlike the urban family, the traditional farm family was thought to be multi-generational, with children learning the trade of farming and eventually inheriting the family operation. Grandparents were valued for their farming knowledge and lived in the household of one of their farming children. In summary, we assume that the roots of the structure of rural families lie in the extended farm household, in which rural seniors lived with their children.

There is some evidence that households of rural seniors were more extended in the past. A comparison of census data from 1900 and 1980 in a rural Kentucky farming community (Arcury, 1984) showed that, in 1900, family size was larger than it was in 1980 and most farm seniors had at least one unmarried child living with them. By 1980 there were fewer extended households and more nuclear family households. The unexpected finding was that during both periods, the majority of elders lived in nuclear family households. By 1980, however, nuclear families were smaller, with few unmarried children remaining in the parental home.

Most contemporary Canadian farm seniors also live in nuclear households **(Table 4.1)**. In fact farm elders are the most 'nuclear' of any group of seniors in Canada. In comparison to both non-farm and urban elders, farm

63

TABLE 4.1

POPULATION OVER AGE 65: CANADA 1986

	Canada	Total Urban	Total Rural	Rural Non-Farm	Rural Farm
People over 65					
Living with spouse and/or unmarried children	61	58	68	67	78
Living alone	28	30	21	22	7
Living with other relatives	10	9	9	9	12
Living with non-relatives	2	2	2	2	7

SOURCE: Statistics Canada (1988d) *Selected Characteristics for Urban and Rural areas, for Canada, Provinces and Territories, 1986 Census-100% data.* Catalogue # 94-129, p. 5.

seniors are most likely to live with their spouse and less likely to live alone. However, they are also most likely to live in some sort of extended household, either with other relatives or non-kin.

These differences in household composition of farm and non-farm rural seniors are still based in the family traditions in agriculture. Elderly farm households are nuclear in part because few women remain on the farm homestead once they are widowed. In many farm operations, widowhood is the signal for the next generation to take on sole operation of the farm and to move into the 'big house'. Most farm widows subsequently move into the nearest town, leaving a lower proportion of nuclear families among farm than non-farm seniors and a higher proportion of singles in non-farm centres **(Table 4.1)**. The majority of farm elders living alone are never-married men.

Family structures of seniors in fishing communities are similar to those in farming. In Newfoundland outport villages, fishing for Atlantic cod also requires high labour inputs. Most operations are run by cooperating groups of kin which may span three generations of fathers, sons, brothers, paternal uncles, cousins plus wives and unmarried daughters and sisters who work in the fishery (McCay, 1987). Despite the economic interconnections in families, extended family households are also uncommon in these communities. Two household structures predominated among retired fishermen in one such community. Most (79 percent) lived in nuclear family households which included unmarried adults who usually lived with their parents. Only if they could not cope on their own, did older people move in with children. The second most common household structure was one in which single men lived alone. Both fishing and farming communities have a tradition of high male-female sex ratios, resulting in large percentages of never-married men. The high percentages of men in these resource-based communities began with migration of young men into these communities in search of work. In recent years, young women have left these communities in search of employment opportunities.

In both farming and fishing communities, most elders live in nuclear families, with higher proportions of unmarried children living with parents in more isolated communities. Elders may live with other relatives if they are unable to maintain their own households. More people living alone in these communities are likely than in other rural areas to be never-married men rather than widowed women (McCay, 1987).

Farm elders in the United States have similar household structures to those in Canada. Data from the 1986 census indicates that rural farm elders are more likely to live in separate dwellings with their spouse (78 percent) than are non-farm (67 percent) or urban (58 percent) seniors (Statistics Canada, 1988d). Also similar to Canada, farm elders are least likely to live alone. Only 17 percent live by themselves as compared to 27 percent of non-farm and 34 percent of urban dwellers (Coward, Cutler and Schmidt, 1988).

By 1986, in Canada, there were no overall differences in family size among rural farm, rural non-farm and urban households. Nonetheless, rural household structures varied in other ways such as household composition, age and gender. Differences in household composition of farm and non-farm households are one such variation, with non-farm households more similar in composition to urban than to farm households **(Table 4.1)**. Non-farm and urban seniors are more likely to live alone and less likely to live with other relatives or non-kin than are farm seniors. Another source of variation is age and gender of the elder. Nuclear family households predominate only among younger seniors. The most common living situation of those aged 65 to 74 is with their spouse, while the largest proportion of those over 75 live with their children (Vivian, 1982).

Household structure is also very dependent on gender. Women have traditionally experienced more changes in the structure of their households than have men. Canadian women are more likely than men to be widowed and to live alone or move into the households of one of their children. Most men continue to live with their spouses until the death of the man (Connidis, 1989). This is a long-standing pattern. Even in 1900, most elderly men remained married, while most women became widowed and moved from being the wife of the household head, to being the parent of the household head and dependents of their children. In 1980, older men were still likely to live in nuclear families, although their households contained fewer unmarried children. Older women were just as likely to become widows but were more likely to live separately from their children (Arcury, 1986).

FAMILY NETWORKS

This examination of the structure of rural households has shown that few rural elders live in extended family households. However, it does not address the question of whether they have larger extended families living nearby than do urban elders, nor whether rural families are more emotionally supportive and close (Wister, 1985).

Canadian seniors in general have large family networks. Approximately 80 percent of all seniors have children, siblings and grandchildren (Connidis, 1989). Although there is some evidence that rural seniors have larger family networks than do urban elders (Deimling and Huber, 1981; Martin Matthews, 1988a), age, cohort and marital status may account for more differences than place of residence. Those over 85 and those who have never married are likely to be without kin. The latter group may be less vulnerable as they age since never-married seniors often compensate for lack of close kin by developing intimate relationships with friends and more distant kin (Connidis, 1989).

Availability of kin is related to the resident's length of tenure. Long-term residents of rural areas are likely to have a relatively stable network size and close-kin membership (Wenger, 1986). In contrast, in-movers such as the Wilsons described in Chapter 1, will have virtually no established kinship network nearby; while those who move to be close to one of their children will have a small local network. Perhaps because of the variation in availability of kin, rural-urban comparisons of network availability have been inconsistent. While urban elders in Saskatchewan are more likely than rural dwellers to have family members nearby (Grant and Rice, 1983), the opposite is true in some communities in Quebec (Corin, 1984; Corin et al., 1984). In other countries such as Wales, no differences have been found between rural and urban areas in terms of availability of family members (Wenger, 1982).

Perhaps a more important difference between rural and urban seniors is that rural elders perceive themselves to be more conveniently situated to friends and family than are their urban counterparts (Scott and Roberto, 1987), regardless of actual distance. One reason for this finding is that many rural seniors grew up at a time when travel was difficult. Better roads and cars make access today much easier. Rural elders are also more likely to stress the importance of their friends and neighbours, especially long-standing associations going back to early adulthood or childhood (Kivett, 1988a; Wood, 1981).

Despite the perception among rural elders that their social network is more accessible, studies of the amount of contact with relatives and friends show few rural-urban differences. Most elderly Canadians see at least one of their children on a regular basis, with other relatives seen much less frequently (Connidis, 1989). Of distant kin, neighbours and friends, neighbours are seen most often (Wenger, 1986). A study of 1200 seniors in Newfoundland and Labrador showed that 50 percent saw at least one child daily, suggesting that even if seniors do not live in multi-generation households, children are close by. Only 11 percent saw other relatives daily and half saw other relatives less than once a month. The majority saw neighbours either daily (35 percent) or several times a week (28 percent) (Vivian, 1982). While some have argued that urban men and women have more contact with friends than do their counterparts in rural areas (Keith and Nauta, 1988), others find that the rural elderly have higher levels of contact with neighbours (Wenger, 1982).

Overall, rural Canadian seniors are as integrated into family and non-family networks as are the urban elderly (Martin Matthews, 1988a). However, the amount of integration into a family network is dependent upon whether the elder is a recent in-migrant or long-term resident (Harper, 1987). Among those who retire to the countryside without local kin, kinship networks are typified by long-distance relationships, with occasional short periods of close family contact. These networks are primarily social, with support and social roles clearly differentiated. Indigenous elderly are more likely to rely on kin for both social contact and support. A broad kinship network and long-term reciprocity allow for support and interaction to be shared. A third group, retired in-migrants with local kin, tend to look to kin for social and practical support. Local kin are often restricted to one child and his/her family, with the move to the countryside precipitated by a family crisis such as retirement or widowhood. Relocation requires a relearning of roles for both generations. This last group is representative of a fairly common retirement pattern in North America. Of a group of elders in the midwestern United States who had moved in the past five years, there were two major reasons for moving: moving from the farm into town, and moving to be closer to relatives (McGhee, 1985).

Despite the stereotype of the large rural extended household, rural seniors are, in fact, most likely to live in nuclear households. However, as with their urban counterparts, most have a network of kin and friends which they perceive to be accessible. A fruitful avenue of investigation would be to study the impact of 'rural type' (defined in terms of household structure, age and gender) on the variety of patterns of contact with kin and non-kin.

FAMILY SUPPORT

One of the major areas of interest in social gerontology is family support, and how the nature of support changes over time in a family. This emphasis arises from the expectation that with age, the older person will have increasingly asymmetrical relationships, typified by a decrease in the amount of affection and affirmation received and an increase in the amount of direct aid received (Black, 1985). The emphasis in the research on the study of provision of direct aid has been unfortunate since it creates the impression that all older people need help (Connidis, 1989). It also means that we know less about affection and affirmation aspects of support than we do about the giving of material or symbolic aid.

The difference between 'support as aid' and 'support as affirmation' is similar to the difference between care and caring. Care is to make provision for. The term is often used in the context of long-term care to the elderly, "an integrated mix of health, psychosocial, support and maintenance services provided on a prolonged basis, either continuously or intermittently, to individuals whose functional capacities are chronically impaired or at risk of impairment" (Alberta Long Term Care Institutions Branch, 1989: 1). In this context, care is given to those who are frail and lack the resources to be involved in symmetrical relationships. In contrast, caring is to be concerned or solicitous and to have affection for an individual and the primary source of caring is intimate relationships. Families might define (long term) caring as "a mix of physical and emotional support provided by families to all family members throughout life" (Keating, 1989). Most family members do not separate caring from care. The important elements of 'support as affirmation' are long-term involvement, reciprocity, the expression of affection, and affirmation or endorsement of another person's behaviour, perceptions or expressed views (Black, 1985).

Support as Affirmation

The Parent-Child Relationship

Although most research on parent-adult offspring relationships has been on the exchange of aid between the generations, a more recent concern has been on the quality of the parent-child relationship and its impact on the life of the parent (Connidis, 1989). One of the theoretical approaches to the study of the quality of parent-child relationships is the "generational stake" (Bengston, 1971). When applied to elderly parents and their adult children, the major hypothesis of this theory is that as parents grow older, their reduced resources and power lead them to have a greater need for the relationship with their children than their children have with them; a higher "stake" in the relationship. This greater need is expected to result in highly positive evaluations by parents of the quality of the parent-child relationship and a reluctance to expect high levels of interaction with the child (Keating and Munro, 1989; Mercier, Paulson and Morris, 1988).

Some support for this hypothesis comes through evidence that most rural (Kivett, 1988b) and urban seniors have a high level of trust in, and positive regard for their children. However, sources of the quality of the relationship differ for urban and rural dwellers. For rural parents, geographic proximity of the child was the best predictor of a high quality relationship from the perspective of the parent. Other predictors of a good parent-child relationships were a high level of parental education, internal locus of control and low filial expectations. For urban respondents, parents with a higher quality relationship were older, lived farther away and had a higher internal locus of control (Mercier, Paulson and Morris, 1988). It seems that parental perceptions of high quality relationships occur when child obligations are low. Thus, for rural seniors, relationships were best when the parent felt she had control over her life; when she did not turn to that child in an emergency; and if she did not have expectations of high levels of interaction, but if the child was available if needed.

Rural seniors in households shared with children have lower morale and perceive relationships with children to be more strained than those in independent households, perhaps because of the interdependence in such households. Those who have higher morale effectively reduce the affirmation obligations of children through high levels of community participation in clubs, organizations or church (Kivett and Learner, 1980).

Not all research points to the relative powerlessness and high stake of rural parents in the parent-child relationship. The economic structure of fishing and farming communities often means that older parents maintain control through continued ownership or management of the business. The poverty of some fishing communities affords another kind of power to retirees. Seniors in Newfoundland outport villages are relatively wealthy because they receive Old Age Security. Through the 'power of surplus cash', seniors develop obligations in others through giving money for services, even those supplied by children (McCay, 1987). Further research on the quality of parent-child relationships from the perspective of these resource-rich parents is necessary to test the relationship between power and generational stake.

Adult children are expected to have less stake in their relationships with their parents but to maintain the relationship because of feelings of obligation and a sense of long-term reciprocity. Among middle-aged children of Mennonite faith in rural Manitoba, Bond and Harvey (1987) found a strong sense of obligation with a 'rule bound' approach to family life. Respondents felt obligated to provide care to family members despite inconveniences. Similarly in a study of rural villages in southern Italy, 72 percent of adult children said they accepted the obligation to share their homes with elderly parents. However, only 28 percent did so voluntarily (Gennaro, 1983). Other North American studies have found that much parent-child contact in rural families occurs at prescribed times such as birthdays, family reunions, other family ceremonies and emergencies, suggesting that a sense of obligation plays a significant role in the association (Kivett, 1988b).

These findings on the quality of the parent-child relationship illustrate how the relationship might vary considerably, depending upon the resources of the elderly parent. Because parent-child relationships are almost invariably asymmetrical, it seems that there should be more potential for high-quality relationships among same-generation peers including siblings, friends and neighbours.

The Marital Relationship

Overall, older Canadians are highly satisfied with their marriages and place high value on emotional security, respect and communication. As they grow older, couples become increasingly interdependent (Connidis, 1989). Interdependence is especially relevant to rural couples whose lives are based on a close partnership in both work and family roles. Farming couples have symmetrical work roles in which both husbands and wives produce goods necessary for the survival of the business and the family (Vanek, 1980). Since business and family roles operate in the same place, tensions often arise over the ability of couples successfully to manage competing roles. An important source of personal satisfaction for farm wives is their husbands' acknowledgement that they have a farm-work-role as well as a family role (Keating, 1987). Throughout a long married life, couples work out the interrelationships between work and family roles. Rural women over 65 are more satisfied with their farm and family roles than their younger counterparts (Keating and Munro, 1988).

Non-farm couples are less likely to be bound together by joint work roles. However, during the post-retirement years they tend to move toward more role integration and less gender differentiation through decreasing the amount of household role segregation (Dorfman and Heckert, 1988). In making these changes, husbands may be compensating for their lost work role by participating in household roles. Or couples may choose to share household tasks in order to spend more time together during retirement. Rural women's retirement satisfaction is related to the proportion of family decisions shared jointly with their spouses (Dorfman and Hill, 1986).

Although it seems as if the marriages of rural seniors are interdependent, these data do not provide a full picture of the relationship of husbands and wives. We still know relatively little about the levels of intimacy in such marriages or the conflicts that may arise from the pressures of working together.

The Sibling Relationship

The sibling relationship appears to have great potential for affection. It is often the first intimate relationship among peers (Connidis, 1989). Of all close kinship ties, the sibling relationship may be the most free, since societal expectations are that it endure but need not be actively pursued. In a review of research on sibling relationships, McGhee (1985) found that sibling contact is not motivated by obligations to keep in touch but by geographic proximity, affectional closeness and enjoyment. She found that bonds among sisters were closest, and that there are great positive benefits of associating with a sibling of the same sex who shares one's history, values and interests. In her study of rural seniors in Indiana, McGhee found that the presence of a same sex sibling was a predictor of life satisfaction for women but not for men. She says that one of the major drawbacks for rural elders in maintaining close sibling relationships is geographic distance.

Support as affirmation appears to be important to the quality of life of rural elders. The way in which affirmation is manifested depends on the type of kinship relationship. Paradoxically, relationships that are less intense such as sibling relationships have more potential for affection without obligation.

Support as Aid

Most Canadian surveys on needs of the rural elderly appear to be under-taken to document unmet needs. Few ask directly whether support or aid is required, although estimates are that between 45 percent and 55 percent of rural seniors either see no need for help (Vivian, 1982) or do not use available services (Newhouse and McAuley, 1987). It is virtually impos-sible with the present state of our knowledge about rural elders to know how many are in need of 'support as aid'. Yet, this documentation is important, since when they need help, rural elders may have to rely more on informal sources than do urban elders who have better access to formal services (Coward and Cutler, 1989).

Both young and old rural Canadians see a hierarchy of obligation to provide aid to elderly family members. Storm, Storm and Strike-Schurman (1985) explored perceived obligations to assist a frail old person with physical care, financial aid and psychological support among a group of women aged 18 to 85. All lived in a small town in the Maritimes. Respond-ents in all age groups saw children as more obligated than other family members to provide aid. Next to children were siblings who, in turn, were more obligated than old friends.

Obligations were not absolute but were lessened by geographic distance and lack of financial resources. Those in the oldest age bracket were more likely to acknowledge conflicting demands which weakened obligations, whereas young adults were more absolute in assigning responsibility to children regardless of special circumstances. Children and grandchildren were thought to have an obligation to visit, call or write regularly, while siblings were much more often mentioned in connection with affirmation than aid. Seniors were seen as primarily responsible for meeting their needs for affection and affirmation through personal initiative and use of their own social resources.

Sources and Types of Support

Data on aid provided to the rural elderly show that there is congruence between attitudes about care and actual amount and sources of caregiving. Data from previous chapters showing that large numbers of elders live independently and have high levels of perceived health, lead us to expect that many elders would see no need for material support. The proportion of rural seniors who say they rely on themselves first, or do not use services, ranges from 28 percent (Vivian, 1982) to over 50 percent (Newhouse and McAuley, 1987). Of those who rely on themselves first, we do not know the proportion who feel free to rely on others if necessary. Nor do we know if non-users are aware of services but do not think they need them; are unaware of available services; or see service use as a personal admission of an inability to cope.

When they receive services from informal sources, rural seniors are most likely to receive aid from children, followed by aid from other relatives and informal sources (Hodge, 1984; Newhouse and McAuley, 1987; Vivian 1982). Rural seniors in the United States tend to receive services if they have poor physical health but good financial and social network resources. A statewide survey of older Virginians analyzed the use of six support areas: telephone and visiting reassurance, continuous supervision, homemaker/ household assistance, meal preparation, nursing care and personal care (Newhouse and McAuley, 1987). High users of in-home services were home-bound because of poor physical health, poor ADL functioning and lack of a car. However, they were likely to live close to a friend and to have good economic resources.

Although there is a commonly held belief that rural elders are cared for by their families more frequently than are urban elders, there are abundant data showing that the majority of long-term care needed by older people in urban Canada is provided by family members (see Connidis, 1989 for a review of Canadian data). Data from rural Canada suggest that this pattern exists there as well. Almost all (75 percent) seniors who say they need help rely on children for that help. Few (5 percent) say they would never turn to children (Vivian, 1982). Help is more likely to be given by daughters to mothers than by sons to fathers (Kivett, 1988b). Perhaps only in remote rural communities do patterns of assistance differ. Studies of geographically remote (Peace River Health Unit, 1986) and culturally remote (Bond and Harvey, 1987; Scott and Kivett, 1980) communities show great emphasis on the provision of family care despite burdens or inconvenience.

The Formal-Informal Provision of Aid

At the beginning of this century our health care services were small in number and modest in scope. Families provided most of the care for ill or frail relatives, in part because there were no alternatives. In the succeeding decades, technological advances and increased sophistication of health and medical services led to greater use of professional and institutional care.

In the past decade we appear to have come full circle. Family-based care is being emphasized again, backed by an ideology in which it is assumed that the family environment is ideal. In its recent policy statement on long-term care, the Province of Alberta states: "It is our view that the new vision for long-term care should aim to foster and promote a continuum of appropriate long term care for the aging population, emphasizing independence and quality of life in a community family-based environment, commensurate with the resources of the province and the individual" (Alberta, Province of, 1988: 9).

The available information on family networks and family support of the rural elderly suggests that most aid is provided in a family-based environment. Yet, the provision of aid by family members, although intuitively appealing, is not without cost to caregivers and recipients. Rural spouse caregivers are likely to have more kin available for support (Deimling and Huber, 1981; Martin Matthews, 1988a) but face personal caregiver costs similar to those of urban caregivers. These include: high levels of caregiver stress, a decrease in social network, lack of respite, a risk to personal health, and feelings of guilt and loss (Johnson and Catalano, 1983; Zarit, Reever and Bach-Peterson, 1980). A substantial proportion (37 percent) of rural residents providing day-to-day care to an ill relative use no relief services, even though the majority (68 percent) say that caregiving has affected their health and that caring for a relative has meant that they could not go away for a vacation (Earle, 1984).

It is assumed that, from the perspective of rural elders, the provision of family-based aid is preferable to formal services. Yet, the norms of intimacy-at-a-distance and the generational stake point to the need for the maintenance of symmetrical family relationships when possible. The use of formal services permits seniors to have more privacy, which is an important value in rural areas. It also allows elders to maintain a level of autonomy in relationship to their informal social network which is not otherwise possible (Corin et al., 1984).

The cultural meaning of the use of formal or informal services may depend on the availability of formal services in the community; personal resources of the senior, ethnicity and type (i.e., age, gender, household composition, etc.) of rural resident. If Corin et al. are correct, when formal services are available, seniors will use them in order to maintain privacy. Thus, services may be used by some seniors who are quite independent and who are able to organize services themselves. They may see this service use as no different than hiring a mechanic to fix the car or a housecleaning service to wash the walls. People like the Wilsons, described in Chapter 1, fall into this group. They are relatively affluent, are skilled in finding and using services, and see themselves as fully in charge of their lives.

Another group of people include those who require somewhat more support, but still are fully in charge of organizing that support. Typical of this group are seniors living in senior citizen apartments in small communities in eastern Ontario (Hodge, 1984). The largest proportions of these residents used two formal services: physician and the Victorian Order of Nurses with small proportions receiving assistance from other formal and informal sources **(Table 4.2)**.

In addition to level of independence, personal resources and skills of the individual also determine how services are used. The use of formal services is associated with a well-developed set of skills in interaction, with involvement in other community activities and with the ability to initiate the use of services themselves (Corin et al., 1984). Those living in seniors apartments may represent a group of seniors who need some aid and have the resources to use that aid. Those who are more frail may have to depend upon their informal network to organize or provide the services they need. This is the group that is especially vulnerable since they rely on their informal network to organize care. Morris and Sherwood (1984) found that the vulnerable elderly in a range of communities from inner-city to rural, used formal help only to fill the gaps in informal help. Only 37 percent of respondents said they had a helper they could rely upon indefinitely, while 87 percent said they had someone they could rely on now and then.

The mix of formal and informal services may also depend on family structure. Retired in-migrants without local kin do not have a well developed, informal 'support as aid' system. Families tend to come together for ritual social occasions and members often find the transition to caregiving problematic (Harper, 1987). In contrast, elders who are indigenous to an area and who have lived in close proximity to family, tend to have relied on kin for affirmation. Because of the close contact, relationships can more easily evolve into the provision of aid as needed. Those who relocate to be near children often do so after a lengthy decision-making process, with the final move often precipitated by a crisis such as widowhood (Rowles, 1983). Children of seniors in this group may feel most pressured to provide aid but feel burdened by disruptions to their lives. Ideally, these families need time to learn new social/affirmation roles before taking on service roles.

SERVICE IMPLICATIONS

The balance of support as affirmation and support as aid is one that families must confront throughout life. When the need for aid is low, this balance seems achievable. Healthy, independent rural seniors generally have strong positive connections to spouses, children and siblings. They seem as well served by an affective system of family and friends as do urban seniors.

TABLE 4.2

ASSISTANCE PROVIDERS TO SMALL TOWN SENIOR CITIZEN APARTMENT DWELLERS

Assistance Providers	% Receiving Assistance
Doctor	62
Victorian Order of Nurses	37
Son/daughter	18
Hired person	17
Community group/service club	16
Friend from community	13
Milkman	11
Friend in building	10
Red Cross homemaker	10
Public health nurse	7
Taxi driver	7
Brother/sister	6

SOURCE: Hodge (1984) *Shelter and Services for the Small Town Elderly: The Role of Assisted Housing*. Ottawa: Canada Mortgage and Housing Corporation, p. 79, Table 5.2.

Those who may not have easy access to affective support are recent in-migrants to rural areas and those who move from farm to non-farm communities, since each of these groups is without a long-standing local network.

Although most support as aid is provided by rural families as it is in urban areas, the rural informal system may be less reliable (Martin Matthews, 1988a), depending upon the type of rural community. Those in farming and remote communities have few formal services to fall back upon and must rely almost exclusively on family and friends. This may place a strain on affective family relationships, although among ethnic groups that place high value on family obligations to provide care, the burdens of care may be taken on willingly, or at least without complaint. Never-married seniors are another special group since they have mostly same-generation kin. As their network ages, there may be few family members able to provide reliable aid when needed. For seniors with financial or land resources, the ability to reciprocate help means that relationships can remain symmetrical. There seems to be little substitution of formal aid for informal aid except among those who are affluent enough and skilled enough to hire formal services as they need them. In general, those who are high users of formal services are also high users of informal help (Beland, 1986).

Although Canadian social policy is moving in the direction of providing a continuum of care in a family-based environment, practice is still oriented toward the individual needing service rather than toward the family of which the individual is a part. Basic to an understanding of the family environment of any senior is an assessment of the family's ability to provide care. A family assessment is essential to understanding the needs and resources of the informal system and should include a social assessment to determine the normative basic, supportive and remedial needs of the individual and the family (Shapiro, 1985).

Depending upon the perceived need of the family for help, practical support to caregivers of such elders can include: training in basic skills necessary to successfully manage the care of rural elders at home; the provision of occasional relief to caregivers; direct financial compensation for caregiving; and the development of lines of communication between formal organizations and agencies and informal caregivers (Newhouse and McAuley, 1987; Tuttle, no date). In-home respite has been rated as the most useful service among rural caregivers with a relative who is cognitively impaired (Tuttle, no date) and has been seen as an essential element of family-oriented policy for the care of Canadian seniors (Olinek, 1989).

SUMMARY AND CONCLUSIONS

Rural Canadian seniors have similar family structures and types of kinship interaction to those of urban seniors. Some differences in structure and interaction between farm and non-farm elders have been found. Non-farm seniors are more likely to live alone than are farm seniors who, if widowed, tend to move off the farm. However, with the decrease in the size of the farm population, comparisons between farm and non-farm elders may be less fruitful than those between other categories of elders such as long-time residents and in-movers. Long-time residents such as Murray Nelson (described in Chapter 1) tend to have large informal networks of friends and relatives, while recent arrivals (like the Wilsons) have to begin to establish an informal network after retirement.

In general, family interaction of rural and urban seniors is similar. The happiest parent-child relationships are in families where children and parents have few obligations to each other. In contrast, families who move to a rural area to be near a child may be vulnerable as the try to establish patterns of both affirmation and support during a crisis period such as bereavement.

Spouses become more interdependent as couples age. However, we know little about levels of intimacy in these marriages, nor about whether couples who work together are likely to have more marital conflict. The sibling relationship has been little studied and may be the one that has the greatest potential to be strong, since it is less intense than other family relationships and there are few expectations about obligations to each other.

Children are seen as most responsible to provide "support as aid" to seniors in need. However seniors' need for "intimacy at-a-distance" and to maintain positive relationships with their children may mean that seniors will choose to use some formal services rather than rely heavily on children. Family care may not always be the best choice.

The question of whether the lack of formal services puts pressure on family caregivers remains unresolved. It seems that when formal services are available they are used to maintain privacy and independence. However, seniors appear relatively unconcerned when formal services are not available. Family research in which caregivers and elders are both asked to comment on lack of formal services would address this question more completely.

CHAPTER 5

HEALTH

In addition to independence, good health is basic to a high quality of life for seniors. Yet, rural elders are often seen as being in poorer health than their urban counterparts and as underserved by health services. In this chapter, definitions of health are reviewed with an emphasis on the way in which health beliefs of rural seniors differ from 'mainstream' definitions. The health status of rural elders is compared to that of urban seniors to shed light on the question of whether rural seniors are in poorer health. Patterns of use of health services by rural seniors, and the perceived adequacy of those services on the part of seniors, provide a basis for assessing whether rural seniors lack adequate health services.

PHILOSOPHIES OF HEALTH AND HEALTH CARE IN CANADA

The way in which a society defines health determines how it assesses health status and organizes health care for its people. Throughout most of the twentieth century, the prevailing definition of health in Canada has been the absence of disease or functional disability (Wilkins and Adams, 1987). This medical model of health emphasizes the amelioration of illness through curative medicine (Torrance, 1987) and was developed in an era when infectious diseases were major killers of adults. Health beliefs consistent with this definition of health include "an acceptance of modern medical science as the basis of valid knowledge in health; a high valuation placed on personal health; a less fatalistic acceptance of disease, illness and injury; a desire for active intervention in illness episodes; and high expectations for good health care" (Torrance, 1987: 7). Health care emphasized curative medicine dispensed through private practice and acute-treatment hospitals. There was little attention paid to prevention, public health or rehabilitation (Torrance, 1987).

The late twentieth century has seen changes in the predominant health beliefs in Canada. Among these is a broadening of the definition of health to "a state of complete physical, mental and social well-being" (Senior Citizens Provincial Council, 1983: 1). Although physical well-being is still central to the new definition, health now has a more positive emphasis on vitality and absence of physical discomfort (Recker and Wong, 1984). Mental health and social health (Goodstadt, Simpson and Loranger, 1987) have been added to the definition.

Concurrent with changes in definitions of health is a shift in philosophies of health care. The new philosophy, known as health promotion, emphasizes "the process of enabling people to increase control over, and to improve, their health" (Epp, 1986: 6). The adoption of the health promotion philosophy marked a shift in attitude away from health care as primarily curative to health care as primarily preventive; and from responsibility for health care as primarily in the hands of health professionals to health care as primarily in the hands of consumers.

Health Goals for Seniors

The past decade has seen a concurrent shift in emphasis toward health care for seniors, with a goal of keeping well and emphasizing alternatives to institutional care (Canada, 1982). Policy statements from Quebec, Ontario, Saskatchewan and Alberta show that these provinces have accepted the health promotion philosophy.

The clearest statement of the proposed replacement of the medical model with a health promotion model of health for seniors comes from The Senior Citizens Provincial Council (1983). The Council stresses the importance of the broader definition of health and the new philosophy of health care. The Council also rejects assumptions that the major element of health care should be disease treatment and maintenance of patients by physicians, hospitals and long-term-care institutions. It states that under the former model of care, frailty and breakdown of the elderly were assumed to be the norm and considered unavoidable by service providers and the elderly themselves. In contrast, the new movement has been towards promotion of optimal well-being, prevention or delay of institutionalization and attending to both social and medical needs of the elderly.

The Alberta Senior Citizens' Secretariat (1986) also endorses the philosophy of health promotion for seniors and states that the philosophy should translate into an approach to health care that prevents unnecessary disability or dependency and ensures that older people can use their strengths and abilities. This theme of taking personal responsibility for health is also evident in the Government of Quebec document on the health of seniors (Quebec Ministry of Social Services, 1985). The Quebec document suggests that major efforts to assist the elderly should not be directed at the elimination of causes of illness, but rather at attempts to mitigate the effects of disease and prevent the loss of autonomy. The authors also say that primary prevention should be aimed at reducing problems such as inadequate housing, social marginalization, and poor nutrition. Secondary prevention should be aimed at alleviating chronic conditions such as loss of autonomy, by promoting physical, social and cultural activities adapted to the needs of the person.

A Government of Ontario document on health strategies for seniors (Office for Senior Citizens' Affairs, 1986) states that the major health goal for seniors is to improve and enhance the quality of life of Ontario's seniors through increased emphasis on health promotion and illness prevention.

These provincial documents indicate that the new philosophy is well entrenched in officialdom. But two questions remain. The first is whether rural seniors hold the same beliefs about health and health care as do health care officials. The second is to what extent these new philosophies are being implemented with rural seniors.

Health Beliefs of Rural Seniors

The health beliefs reviewed in the last section come primarily from health professionals and may not be endorsed by seniors for whom the absence of disease or functional disability becomes increasingly unlikely (Thorne, Griffin and Adlersberg, 1986). Researchers have begun to assess definitions of health held by seniors through the use of qualitative methods in which respondents are asked to develop their own definitions of health. One study of non-institutionalized seniors (Thorne, Griffin and Adlersberg, 1986) found that chronic illness, physical discomfort and functional limitations were only considered important if they affected respondents' abilities to play important roles in their lives. Pain was the one physical health concern that was distinct because of its potential to detract from participation in desired activities.

This theme is also found in the research on rural elders. Using qualitative methods, Weinert and Long (1987) found that residents of rural Montana defined health as the ability to work or to be productive in one's role. Men who had been farmers and ranchers stated that they would tolerate problems so long as they did not interfere with the ability to perform necessary tasks. Women who had been housewives and mothers said that they were healthy when they were able to do what needed to be done.

In a similar study of rural elders in northern Alberta, Raiwet (1989) also found that health was the ability to continue to be involved in the work of farming or trapping and had little to do with chronic physical problems. One respondent saw himself as healthy despite having arthritis which left him with stiff movement, rounded, hunched shoulders and an inability to turn his neck.

> Like I roofed all this trailer and I was up and down them ladders like a jack rabbit. I just took my time and didn't have any accidents. But that's the way it is. You gotta just take your time. Think before you step (Raiwet, 1989: 50).

In contrast is a woman who saw herself as unhealthy despite having no chronic physical problems.

> Well, I don't pick roots no more. I don't trap no more. I used to sew quite a bit on the sewing machine. I used to make moccasins and selling them. I used to but not now. When you can't work anyway, so what's the difference when you die tomorrow or then today? Cause you can't do the things you like to do and a lot of times I sit here and oh boy I'd like to do that and I'd like to work and you can't do it (Raiwet, 1989: 42).

Two other aspects of health identified by rural seniors are maintaining a sense of competence and a sense of meaning. A sense of competence is achieved through remaining involved in all kinds of activities and retaining independence (Thorne, Griffin and Adlersberg, 1986). It also includes taking responsibility for good health by following such practices as: getting enough rest, eating a balanced diet and exercising (Ross, 1984). Having a sense of meaning includes maintaining a sense of self worth (Thorne, Griffin and Adlersberg, 1986) and having feelings such as happiness and contentment (Ross, 1984).

These studies of the ways in which rural elders define good health suggest that health is viewed differently by rural seniors than by those involved in health policy and health service delivery. Rural seniors reject the concept of health as the absence of disease, as do official definitions. But rural seniors seem to fall short of a full-fledged acceptance of health promotion, perhaps because of a realistic perception of what optimal levels of health are for them. Seniors in rural areas may be better able to maintain their sense of being healthy, since the pace of life and of technological change is slower than it is in the city. This makes it possible for people to use familiarity with the setting to compensate for slowed reaction times or failing cognitive abilities (Rowles, 1986).

Personal definitions of good health that are at odds with official definitions may account for some of the discrepancies between objective measures of health status such as chronic illness, and subjective definitions which are individuals' assessments of their own health. As will become evident in the next section of this chapter, most data on the health of all older Canadians still measure illness and functional disabilities.

HEALTH STATUS

Physical Health

One of the major sources of debate about the health of rural seniors is whether their health status is better or worse than the health of those in urban areas. In a review of morbidity data on rural and urban seniors, Martin Matthews (1988a) argues that there are no significant differences in general health between the two groups. Results from provincial research projects across the country support her contention. Studies of the health of seniors in Newfoundland and Labrador (Vivian, 1982), in Alberta (Thurston et al., 1982) and in Ontario (Morton et al., 1984) found no consistent differences in physical health status between the rural and urban elderly.

The majority of seniors in Canada (84 percent of men over 65 and 87 percent of women over 65) have at least one chronic physical problem (Health and Welfare Canada, 1981). Disorders of the circulatory system, cancers and disorders of the respiratory system account for 50 percent of hospitalizations. Problems requiring hospitalization are similar for rural seniors (Senior Citizens Provincial Council, 1983). Of illnesses not requiring hospitalization, the most common among rural seniors is arthritis, with estimates that from 50 percent to 60 percent of seniors suffer from this ailment (Morton et al., 1984; Thurston et al., 1982; Vivian, 1982).

A study of the health status of seniors in Newfoundland and Labrador (Vivian, 1982) is one of the few to compare rates of chronic health problems from the perspective of seniors living in the community and those living in institutions. Rural and urban data are amalgamated with no reported differences between the two groups. **Table 5.1** shows that arthritis is the most common ailment reported by both groups, although institutionalized seniors reported higher incidences of constipation/diarrhea, emotional problems, bladder problems and stroke. Fewer institutionalized respond-

TABLE 5.1

HEALTH PROBLEMS OF COMMUNITY AND FACILITY RESPONDENTS
NEWFOUNDLAND AND LABRADOR

Type of health problem	Community Respondents (N=2240)	Facility Respondents* (N=368)	All Respondents (N=2608)
arthritis	51	53	52
high blood pressure	39	29	38
heart disease	24	26	25
emotional problems	16	23	17
cataracts	14	17	15
constipation/diarrhea	14	30	16
bladder problem	11	24	13
diabetes	11	12	11
stroke	8	17	10
asthma	7	7	7
anemia	5	4	5

*Sample of those who could respond to a questionnaire. Those with cognitive disorders or who are too frail to respond are not represented.

SOURCE: Vivian (1982). *Home Support Services Survey Project*, Vol. 2. St. John's, Newfoundland: Newfoundland Department of Social Services. p. 33, Table 19.

ents have high blood pressure, presumably because this condition is more closely monitored and treated in this group. In this study, only seniors who could respond to a questionnaire were included, so the most frail of community and institutional respondents were not represented.

The one area in which there is some indication of general health status differences between rural and urban seniors is in problems which are amenable to correction if health services are available and used. Rural seniors report more uncorrected problems with vision (Kivett, 1985; Thurston et al., 1982), dental, hearing and foot care problems (Thurston et al., 1982). These differences may be more a function of the lack of available health services than of lower levels of health.

Among seniors, health status is consistently lowest for native seniors, most of whom live on reserves which are culturally and often geographically remote. Mortality data from Saskatchewan indicate that principle causes of death among natives are similar to those of provincial seniors but mortality rates are higher (Gillis, 1987). Diseases related to lifestyle such as, for example, nutritional deficiencies are becoming more prevalent among the native population, while respiratory diseases and accidents related to the environment are on the decline. Morbidity data show that native seniors in northwestern Ontario are prone to nutritional deficiencies such as obesity, iron deficiency anemia and vitamin deficiency (Young, 1987). Native seniors are the group most at risk of poor health among Canada's rural elders.

Morbidity data on rural elders suggests that like urban elders, most have at least one chronic health problem. However, mortality data show that both groups are living longer. In the fifty years from 1930 to 1980, life expectancy of men at age 65 increased by one year from 13 to 14 years. Life expectancy of women increased by four years from 14 to 18 years (Senior Citizens Provincial Council, 1983). Thus, seniors are living longer with chronic health problems. Personal definitions of health become important in terms of how seniors live with long-term chronic problems. 'Less serious' illnesses like arthritis are likely to be seen as more problematic than some diseases which require hospitalization, since these less serious illnesses might have more long term impact on the ability to take part in desired activities.

Mental Health

Much of the research on the mental health of Canadian seniors has dealt with general levels of satisfaction with life, rather than with patterns of mental illness. In a recent review of well-being of older Canadians, Connidis (1987) suggests that Canadian seniors tend to rate themselves high on life-satisfaction.

Despite generally high levels of life satisfaction, some seniors do suffer from poor mental health. Suicide is one of the most common causes of death among senior citizens in Saskatchewan, claiming the same number of lives as motor vehicle accidents among those over 65. Elderly citizens most at risk of committing suicide are men between 65 and 69, living in western Canada, socially isolated and lonely; who have recently experienced a significant loss or change in status, such as widowhood or retirement, are widowed or unattached, live near or below the poverty level, and are in poor physical health. No rural-urban differences are found, nor have reasons for higher suicide rates in western Canada been delineated (Senior Citizens Provincial Council, 1983). This group with very low life-satisfaction often goes undocumented by researchers, who find an overall high-average level of life-satisfaction among seniors.

Overall, rural elders are presumed to have high levels of life satisfaction because of strongly held rural values and because they are close to the land. However, there is a counter-argument that rural seniors may be satisfied with life because they have lower aspirations, a more limited idea of what is possible, or because they are resigned to their fate (Shapiro and Roos, 1984). Rural seniors in some areas report fewer chronic health conditions than do urban seniors and are less apt to have seen a doctor during the past year, or to have been confined to bed because of an illness during the last month. Rural people may not want to be seen as complainers or may be more tolerant of disability (Lubben et al., 1988).

There is little evidence of rural-urban differences in life-satisfaction. Kivett (1985) looked at rural-urban differences in the morale of older adults in a rural transition area in North Carolina and concluded that in rural areas close to urban centres, mental health characteristics were similar to those of adjacent urban elderly.

More promising than rural-urban comparisons in life-satisfaction has been research which attempts to delineate the variation in life satisfaction among rural residents. An innovative study by Scheidt (1984) sheds some light on this issue. Scheidt developed a taxonomy of well-being based on a sample of 990 elderly rural residents aged 65 to 98, in 18 towns with populations of 2500 or fewer in Kansas. He used several measures of subjective well-being (including satisfaction with housing and neighbourhood, extent of visiting with friends and relatives, degree of mobility, functional health, feelings of security) and measures of psychological well being. He found four major patterns of well being: partially engaged, fully engaged, disengaged, and frail.

The partially engaged (46 percent) were the largest group. They had high mental and physical health, took part in relatively few home visits with friends and relatives but were involved in formal and informal town activities. Members of this group tended to be married and well educated. The fully engaged (19 percent) were among the most active and mobile in the community and visited friends and relatives more than did the partially engaged. In contrast, the disengaged (17 percent) were in relatively robust physical and mental health but had a low degree of social activity and community involvement. Finally, the frail (8 percent) had the poorest physical and mental health, and the least social contact and participated least in activities. Most in the 'frail' category reported low morale and greater unhappiness than happiness.

Scheidt concludes that the differences in the pattern of well-being among these rural elders negates both the romanticized and starkly desolate depictions of the rural elderly. Results show systematic variation among older residents of small towns. The majority have high satisfaction and a variety of ways of engaging in the community, while a small proportion are in poor health and are isolated from the community. The latter group have been identified as the most at risk for health problems.

Despite research such as that done by Scheidt, stereotypes about the well-being of rural elders are remarkably persistent. This may be due to the fact that, with the ongoing move away from an agricultural economy, many people have little contact with rural life. It may be part of an urban bias that life must be grim without city amenities or idyllic with family members close by. This is another example of our failure to recognize the heterogeneity of rural seniors.

The Relationship between Physical and Mental Health

Several Canadian researchers have found that a strong predictor of well-being or life-satisfaction is physical health (Gooding, Sloan and Amsel, 1988; Kozma and Stones, 1983; Michalos, 1982). Factors indicating good physical health include: minimal limitation of activity, limitation of short duration, taking few drugs, not having visited a physician in the past two weeks and experiencing few stressful life events. Physical health factors are more important than psychosocial factors in predicting well-being in later years (Gooding, Sloan and Amsel, 1988).

Rural-urban comparisons of predictors of life-satisfaction show good health to be a predominant factor for rural seniors. Kozma and Stones (1983) studied the happiness of 200 urban and 200 rural Newfoundlanders over 64 years of age. Health and marital status were predictors of happiness for rural respondents, while predictors for urban residents were housing satisfaction, health, activities and changes in life events. Farm and non-farm seniors also differed from each other in patterns of predictors of life satisfaction. For farm people, satisfaction with religion, health and housing had the greatest impact on satisfaction. For non-farm seniors, self esteem, housing and health were most important (Michalos, 1982). Another approach to understanding variation in physical and mental health has been to develop typologies of rural elders using both measures. Preston and Mansfield (1984) assessed mental health (i.e., extent to which recent life events were bothersome and coping mechanisms used) and physical health (illnesses experienced) in a sample of 200 rural farm and non-farm elderly over age 60. Like Scheidt, they too found that their sample divided into four groups which differed in stress levels, numbers of coping mechanisms, number of helpers, subjective health status and amount of activity limitation due to health problems.

All of these studies indicate the need to look more at the variation between rural subgroups. Physical health may be a more important predictor of life-satisfaction for people for whom physical activity was an essential part of their work and identity. For others, personal identity and physical environment may be more central. Further exploration of the interaction among these variables will help advance the understanding of the interactions between physical health, perceived health and overall satisfaction with life.

In reviewing the findings on health status, Krout (1988) says that it is impossible to determine the nature or magnitude of rural-urban differences in health with the existing research in that area. Most studies do not use multivariate analyses or controls and there are no consistent definitions of urban or rural or consistent measures of health status. Krout suggests that it would be more fruitful to ask fundamental questions, such as is: Why and how does rural versus urban residence interact with health-related variables? Does living in the midst of a greater or lesser number of people affect an older person's health, and if so, why? Does a smaller population lead to a more dense social network, which creates a greater sense of security and psychological satisfaction and acts as a buffer against physical illness? Does the 'more natural' physical environment positively affect health or negatively affect it through higher risk of accidents, etc? How much do limited opportunities for occupational mobility earlier in life in rural areas lead to lower incomes, lower nutritional levels, lower standard of living and thus lower levels of health? Do rural values of self-reliance lead to lesser likelihood of admitting to health problems, so that only objective measures of morbidity will reveal differences in health levels between rural and urban groups?

TABLE 5.2
SELF-RATED HEALTH OF OLDER CANADIANS

AGE	SELF-RATED HEALTH				
	EXCELLENT	VERY GOOD	GOOD	FAIR	POOR
less than 55	27	39	26	7	1
55-64	20	28	30	14	7
65+	20	26	28	18	8

SOURCE: Reproduced with permission of the Minister of Supply and Services Canada 1991. Health and Welfare Canada (1989). *Active Health Report on Seniors*. Ottawa: Minister of Supply and Services, p. 7, Figure 1A.

Self-rated Health Status

Most older Canadians rate their health as good to excellent (Health and Welfare Canada, 1989; **Table 5.2**), a finding that is surprising in light of the high levels of chronic illness experienced by seniors but congruent with seniors' own definitions of health. Regional studies show similarity in seniors' assessment of their health status. Studies in Alberta, Saskatchewan and Newfoundland have found that 60 to 70 percent of seniors rate their current state of health as excellent or good. Similar proportions rate their health as the same or better than it was five years previously. Even those in institutional settings rate their health quite highly. Half of the institutionalized respondents in studies in Alberta and Newfoundland said their health was excellent or good (Senior Citizens Provincial Council, 1983; Thurston et al., 1982; Vivian, 1982).

Rural-urban comparisons do not show such consistency. While in Alberta there were no significant differences in perceived health status between town and rural elders (Thurston et al., 1982), a Manitoba study found that urban seniors rated their health more highly (Shapiro and Roos, 1984; Thurston et al., 1982). Only one Canadian study found the majority of seniors (54 percent) rated their health as fair or poor. The study was of three rural home care districts (Senior Citizens Provincial Council, 1983). The authors suggest these results are lower than for other studies because a mailed questionnaire was used and respondents felt freer to be honest and not overrate their health. They also note that some of their respondents were quite frail, including 8 percent who could not leave their home without help.

Other studies confirm that not all rural elderly rate their health positively. In a study of widowed black seniors in the rural south, Scott and Kivett (1980) found none who perceived their health as excellent. Twenty five percent rated their health as poor or good and 50 percent as fair. One third said that health problems severely limited their ability to do the things they wanted to do. These findings may reflect the fact that this is an especially deprived group with an average of less than five years education and a mean annual income of $1,990. There are no comparative data on ethnic groups in Canada on this issue.

Rural seniors rate their health more positively than morbidity data would suggest is warranted. Health promotion models are likely to require that more attention be paid to these self-assessments than in the past. Self-rated health is generally more closely correlated than is morbidity with the use of health services, functional abilities, support needed and life-satisfaction (Senior Citizens Provincial Council, 1983). Thus, service deliverers need to take into account people's assessments of their own health as much as they need to attend to professional assessments of functional problems.

HEALTH SERVICES FOR RURAL SENIORS

Health Service Utilization

The question of how well rural seniors are served by health services depends in part upon whether the assessment is based on the 'old' or 'new' philosophy of health care. From the perspective of the old philosophy of treatment of disease through acute-care facilities, seniors are quite well served. Current services to seniors are focused on those who have clearly existing illnesses (Alberta Senior Citizens' Secretariat, 1986). From the perspective of health promotion, fewer systems are in place. The emphasis on keeping well and emphasizing alternatives to institutional care is not widely practised throughout the country (Canada, 1982).

Canadian seniors are heavy users of physical health services but low users of mental health services. A typical pattern is that of Alberta, where seniors use 33 percent of acute care hospital days and 83 percent of home care services, but comprise only 8 percent of the population (Alberta Senior Citizens' Secretariat, 1986). Urban seniors account for much of this high service use, while rural seniors are presumed to be lower users because of the unavailability of services. In the United States there is evidence for this assumption that rural seniors use health services less frequently than do urban seniors. Rural seniors are less likely than urban seniors to receive hospital treatment, or to visit physicians or dentists (Palmore, 1983). They also have access to a narrower range of health services with fewer health-care providers (Coward and Cutler, 1989). Although rural states target higher proportions of their budgets to the elderly, these states have substantially smaller health budgets to work with, resulting in a lower proportional share of public health resources and services (Nelson, 1983). Rural seniors in the United States appear to be disadvantaged in terms of health services.

Canadian data are more equivocal and the level of service use varies according to the type of service, region of the country and ethnicity of the user group. Several Canadian studies have pointed to a lack of physicians in rural areas. In rural Manitoba there are fewer physicians than there are in urban areas and use of physician services is in proportion to their availability. Rural seniors of all age categories make significantly fewer physician visits per year than do their urban counterparts (Shapiro and Roos, 1984).

Low numbers of physician visits were also found in a study in the Peace River district of Alberta. Fewer residents of remote parts of the district (26 percent) than residents of small communities (43 percent) had made physician visits during the past year (Peace River Health Unit, 1986). Regional studies such as one done in North Frontenac, Ontario by Chamberlain (1976) provide anecdotal evidence of a lack of physician services. The authors state that there was only one full time physician in the area and that the only other physician services were provided by a non-resident physician who owned a cottage and saw patients on weekends during the summer.

In contrast to physician availability, some areas of rural Canada are well-served by hospital facilities. In rural Manitoba there are more hospital beds than there are in urban areas (Shapiro and Roos, 1984). Again, use of these services is in proportion to their availability, with higher numbers of hospital days per year for rural seniors of all age categories. Seniors in remote areas do not fare as well. In northern Alberta, 55 percent of seniors living in small communities versus 46 percent of those in more remote areas had stayed in a hospital in the previous year (Peace River Health Unit, 1986). Native elders also have high rates of hospitalization. Older Native people in Saskatchewan are almost three times as likely as non-Native seniors to be hospitalized (Gillis, 1987). Native elders are more frequently admitted to hospital for diagnostic purposes. The most frequent cause of hospital admissions among elderly registered Band members in Saskatchewan in 1986 was "symptoms, signs and ill-defined conditions".

More hospital use among rural seniors is probably not due to poorer health status since rural residents have slightly better survival rates than do urban elderly. Rather, rural poverty may make home treatment a less viable option and lead a physician to admit patients to hospital more often than might otherwise happen. Large travel distances to health care services and transportation problems in a province with long cold winters may also encourage in-hospital treatment. And finally, the greater availability of hospital beds in rural areas may encourage admissions (Shapiro and Roos, 1984).

Rural seniors and seniors in Indian reserves use fewer out-patient or in-patient mental health services than do seniors in any other residential group (Gillis, 1987). It seems unlikely that this low service use reflects decreased need since native elders in particular have higher rates of morbidity than do other seniors. Lack of access to services and greater unwillingness to use services because of the stigma of mental illness seem more likely reasons for non-use. Another possibility is that many mental health problems are dealt with by use of medication. Anxiety, an important predictor of both prescription and non prescription drug use (Sharpe, Smith and Barbre, 1985), does not predict use of mental health services. Of a group of 1000 small town rural elderly in Kansas, only 2 percent of the vulnerable group who had the lowest morale had used mental health services (Windley and Scheidt, 1983).

Native elders are the most disadvantaged of rural seniors in terms of most health services. Although native seniors living on reserves have the same health care coverage (Alberta Health Care and Blue Cross) as do non-natives, natives are deprived of good, responsive health care (Hohn, 1986). There are virtually no nursing homes or auxiliary hospital beds on reserves and almost none exist that cater to the particular needs of older natives. Putting a native relative in a nursing home is often seen as unthinkable by family members. Great distances to travel, lack of staff who speak native languages, unfamiliar food and lack of contact with families are barriers to the use of nursing homes by native seniors. Speaking of native elders in Alberta, Hohn (1986: 33) says, "their real freedom to seek out services may be the most restricted of any group of seniors in the nation".

The lack of adequate health services for native seniors is also evident in data from Manitoba. In a comparison of native and non-native rural elders, Bienvenue and Havens (1986) note that the native population report a lack of access to medical, nursing, dental and eye care. One third of the native elderly, in comparison to 11 percent of non-natives claim they do not have a regular family physician. Thirty-three percent of the native sample compared to six percent of the non-native group claim that medical and nursing care at home were needed but not available. Natives also experienced more unmet needs than non-natives in dental care (35 percent versus 11 percent) and eye care (37 percent versus 11 percent).

> Clearly the native elderly do not receive the health care services which are normally available to other rural Manitoba residents. Whether as a result of distance, communication problems or transportation, the native elderly report a great degree of dissatisfaction with the availability of existing health care services (Bienvenue and Havens, 1986: 245).

Health services to native elders are also under review because the philosophies of health of native people are not the same as those of the dominant culture. In Alberta, The Indian Health Care Commission was established in 1980 after an all-chiefs conference saw the need to improve the health conditions of Indians throughout the province. One of its objectives is to assist Bands in the development and implementation of health care programs that are in keeping with a traditional native perspective which views health in a holistic manner and to encourage the increased influence of elders and traditional healers in maintaining the strength of native culture and traditions (Alberta Indian Health Care Commission, no date).

Also disadvantaged in terms of health services are others who live in remote areas. Not only is there a lack of choice within any one service (Coward and Cutler, 1989), some services are simply unavailable. Services such as Meals-on-Wheels, mental health or drop-in centres are much less available to those in remote areas than to those in small communities (Peace River Health Unit, 1986). The Northwest Territories provides few formal outreach services because it is difficult to attract health professionals to the north. The mandate has been to use the limited professional resources to provide acute care and some public health care, with few resources designated for health promotion. Home care is seen as an urgent need in the Northwest Territories because of the variety of living styles in the north.

Given the fact that seniors are more likely to have traditional patterns of living and that different parts of the Arctic have quite different customs, it is hazardous to attempt to plan health care without seeing people in their home situations (O'Neil, 1987). Community-based services may be more appropriate to deal with the variety of living situations than are institution-based programs. However, many community services such as adult day care are relatively new and most have been set up in urban areas (Alberta Senior Citizens' Secretariat, 1986).

No general comment can be made about the adequacy of formal health services to rural seniors. While some services such as rural hospitals are available, there is often a shortage of physicians to staff those hospitals, and there are great regional and ethnic differences in adequacy and appropriateness of health services In remote areas, seniors use acute care services and have access to almost no preventive health services.

Health Service Needs

By many of the objective measures discussed above, rural seniors are poorly served by health services. However, the variety of health needs in different parts of rural Canada and the differences in perceptions of what is health, mean that there is no clear way to determine whether seniors have unmet health service needs. Perceived availability and appropriateness of services; culture and ethnicity; length of rural residence; and whether services needs are based on medical or health promotion philosophies all affect whether services are seen as appropriate and available.

Perceived Need and Service Availability

Perceived need for services by rural seniors does not always correspond closely to objective measures of service availability. In fact, seniors who are most remote from services often express low levels of need. Only 7 percent of seniors in the Peace River Alberta study discussed earlier reported difficulties with access to services, despite the fact that they were remote from service centres.

Even though rural elders may not be well-served by medical services, they may not acknowledge their health care needs because they do not want to move. For Peace River elders living in remote areas, staying in their own homes is of paramount importance. The majority said that they would be unwilling to move to an institutional setting under any circumstances. Said one respondent, "I'll live where I am until I die" (Peace River Health Unit, 1986: 68). There were no extended care facilities in that area and leaving the community was seen as too emotionally costly. In contrast, 84 percent of town elders said that if necessary they would move to an institution outside of their community. Although remote seniors may be underestimating

TABLE 5.3
PERCEPTIONS OF AVAILABILITY AND NEED FOR HEALTH-RELATED SERVICES COMPARED BY URBAN OR RURAL STATUS OF RESPONDENT

| | Status of the Respondent | | |
| | Urban | | Rural |
Type of service	% who believed service was available in their community	% who believed they needed the service	% who believed service was available in their community	% who believed they needed the service
family doctor	93	43	50	50
specialist MD	72	10	2	7
pharmacist	68	56	65	66
home nursing	88	17	53	14
dentist	62	13	45	10
physical therapist	71	11	15	10
social services	70	9	35	14
financial help	61	5	33	22
counselling	71	2	17	5
meal service	73	9	41	12
transportation	67	18	22	15
homemaker	65	6	3	0
day care	70	0	14	0

SOURCE: Reprinted with permission from the American Geriatrics Society, ("Perceptions of Urban versus Rural Hospital Patients about Return to Their Communities") by (Costello et al.), (*Journal of the American Geriatrics Society*, Vol. 25:552-555, p. 554, Table 1, 1977).

their needs, they may also be making a conscious choice to avoid institutional services.

Perceived need for services and service availability is influenced in other ways by rural beliefs. Rural elders have a different concept of distance than do urban dwellers. Three miles to the nearest neighbour and 200 to 900 miles to the dialysis centre for kidney patients may be seen as manageable (Weinert and Long, 1987). Different concepts of distance may help account for findings of high levels of perceived access to services by a group of male patients over age 65 who were about to be discharged from hospital to their homes (Costello et al., 1977). Information was sought regarding their feelings about availability of and need for 13 health-related services in their local communities. Comparisons were made between those in communities of less than 5000 and those in larger towns or cities. **Table 5.3** shows that in almost all instances, perceived availability was higher for those living in urban areas. However, for both urban and rural respondents, perceived availability almost always exceeded perceived needs.

Flaskerud and Kulz (1984) found the same trend when asking about mental health service needs. About 75 to 80 percent of respondents indicated that their household had little or no need for any of the services they were asked to rate. Ten percent indicated a strong need for all services and another 10 to 15 percent indicated some need. The authors concluded that rural residents do not express a greater need for mental health services than do urban residents.

Culture and ethnicity are also important factors to take into account when considering service needs. The culture of rural communities may preclude easy acceptance of some types of services, such as those for mental health problems. Lack of education among rural residents about emotional disorders and psychiatric care and fear of being identified as someone who has mental problems may preclude the use of such services (Berry and Davis, 1978). Other problems with the acceptance of mental health services may be endemic to the acceptance of other types of health services. Urban born and trained professionals may be viewed as unable to be responsive to rural cultural beliefs or practices. As well, many rural areas have a number of small towns with only one service centre. Those in adjacent towns may not see the service as theirs. The rural tradition of family involvement in care of the elderly may be problematic if a client's family is uncooperative.

Other services that may be appropriate and accepted in some rural communities may be inappropriate in others. In many rural areas Meals on Wheels is considered an essential and very economical service in support of good nutritional health. However, O'Neil (1987) states that Meals on Wheels is unavailable and may not be appropriate in most parts of the Northwest Territories where people prefer local food which is usually shared. Most often family or visitors prepare food for those who are not able to prepare it themselves. The author felt that most families looked after their elderly. When this was not possible, a homemaker was seen as more beneficial than Meals on Wheels. A homemaker could prepare meals especially for the elder using her own community produce.

Rural communities that are stable in population mix have the best opportunity to develop appropriate health services over time. However, retirement communities that have large groups of retirees moving into the area, often are unprepared to cope with an increased need for services as the large population of retirees grows older. One such community in Ontario has 1600 residents in 950 single-family modular housing units (Break, 1985). Almost 80 percent of the respondents said that if their health deteriorated they would stay in the community if they could receive the home care they required. Approximately 16 percent used services that provide assistance at home and in the retirement community. Two full time nurses from the Victorian Order of Nurses had been assigned to the nearest health unit, and increased demand was felt by local homemaking services.

The majority of rural seniors perceive that services available in their communities meet or exceed their needs. Yet some communities are underserved by urban standards, while others are receiving services inappropriate to the rural culture in which they are located. Two groups that warrant further study concerning appropriate type and level of services are remote seniors and those who have moved into retirement communities.

The Wilsons and Murray Nelson represent these two groups of seniors. Ruth and Al Wilson have moved to Kaslo, B.C. which is several hundred km from a large medical centre. Both see themselves as being in good health, although each has a chronic health problem. Ruth suffers from hypertension and Al has diabetes. The Wilsons still look to Vancouver as their medical service centre. They return to Vancouver twice a year for treatment and are in contact by telephone when they have questions about their health. As long as they do not suffer from acute conditions, and as long as they feel healthy, they are adequately served by health services.

Murray Nelson sees Kaslo as his medical service centre. He rarely sees a physician and accepts his arthritis and poor vision as part of growing older. Since neither prevents him from going about his daily activities, he too thinks of himself as healthy. Murray is probably more vulnerable if he has a health problem since he has neither the resources nor the inclination to travel to a distant location for treatment. He has avoided having cataract surgery because the nearest hospital is 100 km away, in a town that he rarely visits.

Promoting Better Health for Rural Seniors

There are several methods to determine the need for health services. Most common are morbidity measures and needs assessment surveys (Flaskerud and Kuiz, 1984). Morbidity measures are most appropriately used to determine the need for amelioration of health problems. They are based on incidence levels of illness measured as number of cases being treated. The major disadvantage of this approach is that the validity of making inferences from cases under treatment to the needs of the general population of an area is questionable (Flaskerud and Kuiz, 1984). It is certainly the case with the rural elderly who are not great users of many services. Needs assessment surveys can be useful if consumers are asked directly to identify their health needs. If a need is not perceived, presumably a service will not be used (Flaskerud and Kuiz, 1984).

There is no doubt that, based on morbidity measures, some groups of rural seniors have poor objective health status and have inadequate health services. For those seniors, better basic health services are warranted. However, only a small proportion of variation in health is determined by service delivery (Alberta Senior Citizens Secretariat, 1986). Equally important are lifestyle factors such as cigarette smoking, poor nutrition, lack of exercise and chronic stress (Lubben et al., 1988). Health promotion programs have been suggested as tools for encouraging productive old age and healthy lifestyles. Two principles are important in developing such programs and increasing the chances of their acceptance. The first is that rural seniors' definitions of health must be taken into account. The second is that program development in rural areas must be undertaken with a view to engaging the acceptance of both rural professionals and rural seniors (Berry and Davis, 1978).

Rural seniors' definitions of health are oriented toward being productive and health promotion must address the issue of work (Weinert and Long, 1987). A health education campaign related to hypertension should emphasize the potential danger of stroke and long-term disability rather than the opportunity for a more comfortable, longer life. Since work is of major importance, health care delivery must also fit within work schedules. Offering health care programs or clinics during peak times in the rural economic cycle, such as haying or calving seasons is self-defeating, even for retired seniors who may be providing support to children during those times (Weinert and Long, 1987).

Developing programs in rural areas that are accepted by rural professionals and seniors is also fundamental to their usefulness. Townsend et al. (1988) report on a model for the development of one such program. Theirs was a community occupational therapy service intended to meet the needs of disabled and elderly citizens in a rural community in Nova Scotia. They recommended a three-phase program development strategy which could be used in most health promotion programs. Phase one involved collaboration with interested professionals in the community. They began with informal discussions with hospital administrators who collaborated with occupational therapists to write a proposal describing the existing occupational therapy services in rural areas and preliminary needs assessment findings from a medical record review of the three hospitals in the area. Phase two was a ten-week pilot project conducted with funding from the existing budgets of the three participating hospitals. Its purpose was to refine the model of service delivery to meet the needs of users and to work with the relevant service teams in the hospital and surrounding communities. In-service sessions were held with administrators, nursing staff, physiotherapists, physicians, community health nurses, social service workers, dieticians, drug dependency counsellors, speech pathologists and others to inform them of the findings. Phase three involved further program development and development of program evaluations which would meet the needs of decision makers and would provide the type of information needed to apply for ongoing funding for the service.

The authors felt that collaboration gave the community both the control and the resources to explore its need for a health-care service that was previously unavailable. The pilot project approach allowed time for the completion of a needs assessment and refinement of a service delivery model applicable to the community. Evaluation was designed specifically to answer questions of accountability anticipated from the community and government in considering a full-time ongoing service.

SUMMARY AND CONCLUSIONS

Our knowledge of the variation in health status of rural seniors remains limited. Overall, rural seniors appear as healthy as urban seniors with some notable exceptions in remote areas of the country. Most rural seniors have at least one chronic health problem, although all seniors are now living longer despite these problems. There has been little research on the mental health of rural seniors. Although most rural seniors rate their life-satisfaction as high, a small but significant proportion has low mental and physical health. This is another indication of the heterogeneity of rural seniors.

The health beliefs of rural seniors are much like the new philosophy of health promotion and most rural seniors see themselves as healthy. The ability to take part in important roles is more central to seniors' ideas about health, than chronic illness. Self-rated health is higher than one would expect from morbidity data. It may be that rural seniors are able to adapt to many physical limitations and therefore can maintain their concept of themselves as healthy. Native seniors and those living in remote areas have lower self-rate health, higher rates of hospitalization and few health-promotion services. These two groups appear to be the most needy in terms of health services.

Discussion in this chapter has not dealt with the question of how much informal services substitute for formal services. This is especially important information, given that it appears that rural residents do have a narrower range of available services. If informal services substitute adequately for inadequate or unavailable formal services, then there may be little negative health outcome for rural seniors. This question was addressed in the chapter on family and social networks. Although families are the first source of support, formal and informal services are not always interchangeable. Planning health programs for rural areas requires that professionals understand seniors' definitions of health, are aware of the extent to which existing services are accessible and are aware of the preferred mix of formal and informal help preferred by elders.

CHAPTER 6

DIRECTIONS FOR RURAL RESEARCH, POLICY AND PRACTICE

In the preceding chapters, various facets of rural aging have been examined. Canadian rural elders have been shown to vary greatly in the extent of their work involvement and in their leisure patterns; in the quality of their near-environments and the level of their integration into the community; in health status and attitudes toward health; and in family and social networks. The heterogeneity of rural elders has not previously been adequately acknowledged, especially in the planning and delivery of social programs and in the development of rural social policy. Because definitions of rural are diverse, research findings are difficult to compare. The purpose of this chapter is to reconsider the definition of rural aging in light of research topics and methods that are influenced by the definition chosen. As well, an analysis of current approaches to needs assessment and service delivery is undertaken. Suggestions for directions in Canadian rural social policy are also included.

RURAL AGING REDEFINED

The debate concerning what is "rural" has been summarized in Chapter 1. Although theoreticians have argued for a more clearly articulated and inclusive definition of rural, such a definition has not been well integrated into research on rural aging in Canada. As one set of researchers has said in frustration, "failure to identify criteria for the definition of rurality is inexcusable and easily rectifiable" (Martin Matthews and Vanden Heuvel, 1986). Specifying a set of criteria for what is rural is certainly possible. Arriving at a consensus on that set of criteria may be more difficult.

Rather than write another general description of what should be included in a definition of rural, it seems more fruitful to discuss facets of the rural experience which could provide direction to researchers attempting to understand the experience of aging in rural Canada. In the first section of this chapter the definition of rural is re-examined in light of its usefulness in understanding the lives of rural elders. Of the three initial components of the definition, a recommendation is made to discard the occupational

criterion and to expand the population density and rural ideology components. A historical perspective is suggested as a means of understanding the
impact of rural communities on the experiences of aging.

Occupation

The origins of rural Canada lie in agriculture. European immigrants came
to the country because of land, and most workers were involved in agriculture
or related industries. Although the numbers of Canadians involved in
agriculture have declined over the past 100 years, it was not until 1961 that
Statistics Canada developed a two-category designation of rural: farm and
non-farm. This change was an important step in the acknowledgement that
the majority of rural Canadians are no longer involved in farming.

Although of historical relevance, occupation is no longer a useful way to
determine which elders are rural and which are not. The two-category
occupational designation is an improvement but its continued focus on
agriculture has led to a failure to examine the range of occupations of rural
dwellers. It has precluded an understanding of the work and retirement of
rural elders in occupations other than agriculture (Krout, 1988) and has left
us without contemporary analyses of the impact of manufacturing and
service industries upon rural communities (Newby, 1986). Occupation
must be abandoned as a facet of the definition of rural, since there is no
longer a single rural occupation to which others can be compared. Occupation should take its place as one of the variables which explain the heterogeneity of rural seniors.

History

Rather than use occupation as a determinant of rurality, aspects of the
history of a community might be more profitably used as part of the
definition of rural. The length of time a community has been settled varies
greatly in Canada, and length of settlement may affect experiences of aging.
From a historical perspective, communities could be placed on a continuum
from longest to most recently settled. At the 'most rural' end of the
continuum are communities that have been settled the longest, allowing
most time for a local culture to develop. This historical definition of rural
would allow for an examination of issues such as the place of seniors in a
community throughout its history; or, for example, the relative difficulty
for a senior of moving into a small community in Quebec where there has
been settlement for over 300 years, versus a newly built retirement community in Manitoba.

Length of settlement can also be determined on a personal level. Martin
Matthews and Vanden Heuvel (1986) have argued that the length of time a
person has been resident in a rural area should be another measure of

rurality, although they are reluctant to state how long is long enough. Discussion earlier in this book suggested that being rural-reared may make the critical difference between those who settle happily into the countryside after retirement and those who do not.

These two historical criteria of rural would encourage further exploration of rural culture and the place of older people in that culture. It would also allow for another approach to examining the idea that rural residence affects one's perspective of aging.

Population Density/Distance

The census definition of rural has been the most common measure of population density. Its major advantage is that it provides categories of community size as well as a cut-off point between rural and urban communities. Some theorists have argued that population density should be considered as a continuum from urban to rural-farm, with rural residence only defined in relation, to urban residence (Coward and Cutler, 1988). This point of view has not been widely accepted. Rural-urban comparisons are seen as impediments to the discovery of unique aspects of rural experience, since everything is conceptualized through urban eyes (Windley and Scheidt, 1988). Urban perspectives also preclude comparisons between rural areas within a given country, between nations, or within nations across different historical periods (Krout, 1988). If "urban" is the standard, then comparisons between categories of "rural" are seen as irrelevant. As a means of determining what is rural, the population continuum has been described as static; useful to describe population size but not to discriminate between people living in areas of different population density (Newby, 1986).

An additional problem with the "population continuum" approach as proposed by Coward and Cutler (1988) is that population density is confounded with occupation since "farm" is used as the most rural end of the continuum. By using "farm" rather than population density, those who live in the open countryside but are not farmers are eliminated from consideration.

A "population continuum" approach can be used under three conditions to measure what is rural. First, population density, not occupation must be the criterion. Thus, a designation like "open countryside" must be substituted for "farm". Second, urban must not always be the standard against which areas with lower density are judged. This frees researchers to make other population density comparisons such as between seniors in different occupations (such as farming and fishing) who live in 'rural' areas of similar size. Finally, two additional population criteria must be added to population density. The most important of these in terms of rural aging is the proportion of the elderly in an area. While the general population density variable allows for an examination of the degree to which the whole population is rural, the aged population density variable would allow for an examination of the degree to which the senior population is rural. It seems likely that an older person in a town of 2000 people in which 30 percent of the population is over age 65, might have a different experience of aging than one living in a town of 2000 where the average age is 30. Finally, distance from population centres also needs to be part of the population density aspect of rural. Geographic distance from service centres may make the experience of aging quite different in communities with otherwise similar population characteristics.

Rural Ideology

There is an assumption that there is a rural ideology which separates rural from non-rural people. Some aspects of this ideology have been discussed in this book, although there has been no systematic examination of the beliefs that constitute the rural ideology. Nonetheless, researchers point to the need to identify life-orienting themes of rural elders (Shenk and McTavish, 1988) and have argued that what is rural can only be determined from the perspective of those who are growing old (Rowles, 1988).

It is time to undertake a systematic mapping of the beliefs of rural elders. It may be that of all aspects of the rural experience, the phenomenology of aging in rural areas holds the key to understanding the diversity of rural aging. In addition to considering life-themes of those in rural areas, it would be useful to know how central are things rural to those living there. Rowles (1988: 121) says that "the experience of aging is 'rural' only inasmuch as the individual understands (even implicitly) rurality to be an integral component of his or her life experience". Thus, the understanding of rural ideology needs to be broadened to take into account the range of life themes of seniors and the phenomenology of "rural".

Figure 6.1 summarizes the facets of "rural" which could provide the basis for the investigation of rural aging. Some of these elements are already well defined. Both population density and historical data can be readily obtained from census data and historical documents such as land titles. Our knowledge of the components of "rural ideology" is not well developed and the usefulness of the 'rural ideology' construct is yet to be determined. In the next section of the chapter, a research agenda based on these facets of 'rural' is proposed.

RESEARCH DIRECTIONS

No single method is likely to be able to fully address the range of questions that arise when studying the heterogeneity of rural aging. Rather, it will

FIGURE 6.1
ELEMENTS OF RURAL AGING

Population density/distance
• population density
• proportion of elders in community
• distance from nearest service centre

History
• length of settlement of the community
• length of time elder has lived in the area

Rural ideology
• life – orienting themes of rural elders
• rurality as integral to the life experience of the elder

---

continue to be necessary to use a variety of methods and disciplinary approaches to understand the complexity of rural aging. The following is a brief review of some of these research issues and approaches.

Research Issues in Population Density Aspects of Rural Aging

Although census data provide some information on characteristics of rural seniors, we need further documentation of the macro-ecological characteristics of rural communities. Demographic information on size of communities and proportions of elders in these communities is obtainable from census data. However, a reframing of current categories is necessary, with farm seniors placed in the same category as non-farm seniors who live in low density areas. Data on occupations of rural seniors, including those in farming, should be part of labour force statistics.

Distance from major population centres is also measurable, although agreement needs to be reached on what is considered a major population centre. Characteristics of the nearest population centre such as availability of basic services have been shown to be important to the lives of rural seniors. Several measures of distance may ultimately prove to be useful, depending upon the aspect of isolation/access that is most important to the question being asked. Actual distance in km to the nearest large community; actual distance to basic services such as health clinics or grocery stores; and distance to the preferred service centre are all elements of distance.

This demographic information will be useful primarily to describe aspects of the rural environment. However, a more fundamental question is whether there is a relationship between population density and experiences of aging. The use of population density characteristics to understand aging has been criticized as "ecological fallacy". The critique is levied at researchers who equate the environmental context with the experiences of individuals whose lives are framed in a personal context (Rowles, 1988). Yet others contend that perceptions of seniors vary by population density and that size of community is an important variable (Windley and Scheidt, 1988). Although it may be a fallacy to equate the rural environment with a set of experiences of aging, the nature of the relationship between the rural environment and the experience of aging is researchable. With well-defined, consistent, macro-level population data, it is possible to begin to assess differences between rural centres varying by population density, proportion of seniors and distance to service centres, to see how these relate to various experiences of aging.

Research Issues in Historical Aspects of Rural Aging

The length of time a community has been established could provide another basis for understanding the lives of rural seniors. A basic question to be addressed by historical analyses of rural communities is what aspects of the history of a community influence the current situation of its elderly residents. Independent variables could include economic stability, major sources of employment, proportion of seniors in the community, and patterns of migration. Several methods and sources are appropriate to gather such information. These include land title searches, local history books, oral histories of long-time residents, and content analyses of local publications such as newspapers.

Land title searches provide information on patterns of settlement and transfer of property. The type of transfer and propensity to transfer property to family members can also indicate aspects of generational relationships in families. In conjunction with analyses of wills, land title searches provide information on the wealth and influence of older people in the community. Patterns of land transfer often determine the size of the extended family in the local area. In areas where land is transferred intact to one child, other children often leave the community to find work elsewhere.

Local histories written by community residents provide information on community topics and people seen to be important by current residents. In conjunction with oral histories of long-time residents, they are an excellent source of information about the culture of the community. Content analyses of local newspapers, especially editorials, can show political beliefs and connections of the community to the greater political and regional milieu, while content analyses of the language used in life histories can illustrate differences between those from open country and residents of villages and small towns (Shenk and McTavish, 1988).

Like the information on population density, much of the historic data on a community is descriptive. This background information can also be used to ask more basic questions such as what the factors are that influence perceived adequacy of retirement income of rural seniors. For instance, long-time residents of Kaslo, which has a history of underemployment, may have much more modest expectations about retirement income than do residents of farming communities where access to large markets and good farming conditions have resulted in comfortable lives for community residents. Historical data can be used to track changes in rural culture over time or to explore the bases of regional differences in attitudes toward aging.

Studying the history of elderly individuals may also be useful to understanding their experience of aging. For example, the number of years a senior has been resident in a community may be one useful indicator of that individual's level of integration into the community. Research using length of residence as a variable has begun to illustrate differences in the experiences of those who have aged in place, in-migrants who are returning home and those who are coming to a rural area for the first time. The latter group are less likely to be fully integrated into local support networks and lack the accumulated social credit and earned status in the community that provide the context for assistance available to lifelong residents.

The relative importance of years of residence in explaining variation in lives of rural elders needs to be further explored. Years of residence may affect adoption of new leisure pursuits, since an individual who is familiar with services and who has a peer group that takes part in the activities is more likely to adopt new leisure activities. Those who have lived longest in a community may be most influenced by community standards and expectations and behave in a more normative manner than recent arrivals. In turn, years of residence may affect the nature of the community itself, since large numbers of new arrivals may change dominant beliefs and strain existing facilities.

Research Issues in Rural Ideology

If "rural" is viewed as a phenomenological perspective of those who are growing old, then rurality must not be seen as an objective circumstance outside the individual, but as an internal creation, an element of the way in which individuals organize and construe their lifeworlds. Qualitative methods can be used effectively in research on rural ideologies since the purpose of these methods is to build theory inductively, starting with the experiences of the people of interest. (See Reinharz and Rowles, 1988, for an excellent review of qualitative methods in aging).

One qualitative method is ethnography, in which the researcher "participates, overtly or covertly, in people's daily lives for an extended period of time, watching what happens, listening to what is said, asking questions; in fact collecting whatever data are available to throw light on the issues with which he or she is concerned" (Hammersley and Atkinson, 1983: 2). Ethnography has been seen as a useful method to learn more about the culture of the rural elderly (Krout, 1988; Rowles, 1988). It could also be used to get at predominant values among seniors in a variety of communities that vary in size, degree of isolation and history. These data could then form the basis for the development of general principles on the nature of values and beliefs of rural seniors.

There are many aspects of rural ideology that require documentation. An understanding of the nature of the 'independent rural personality' might help policy makers determine what kinds of services would be used by rural seniors. Knowledge of the extent to which rural dwellers value close-knit communities might help researchers predict the degree of difficulty faced by recent retirees entering the community. Another aspect of rural ideology seen as fundamental to rural life is the 'domestic idyll' according to which the rural woman is expected to stay within the home as the linch pin of the community. An examination of the way in which the "domestic idyll" shapes the lives of rural women could be of special interest to feminist researchers attempting to understand the place of older women in rural communities. Little (1986) argues that this rural value places women outside the hierarchical structures of power and public status which have evolved within the rural community, with the result that problems of rural women are unlikely to receive much attention. The "domestic idyll" might put older women in double jeopardy if they are already marginalized because of their age.

SERVICE DELIVERY

Determining Service Needs

One of the major practice issues in rural gerontology is that of determining service needs of rural elders and developing service delivery models to achieve those needs. This has proved to be a complex task. One of the paradoxes of rural aging is that seniors do not see their lives as particularly problematic despite the fact that many needs assessments show objective disadvantages.

Methods of formal needs assessment are well developed. However, although there have been many needs assessment studies of the rural elderly, these studies have lacked methodological clarity, leaving the reader unsure of both the assumptions on which the research is based, and the validity and reliability of the findings.

Needs assessments require two types of information: the desired state of affairs (goal) and the way in which the actual state of affairs relates to the goal (need) (Krout, 1988). Weaknesses in many needs assessments lie in the way goals are determined. It is often unclear whether the stated goals are those of professionals, or those of rural seniors themselves. This is the source of many of the problems in interpreting findings from needs assessments. If researchers hold an implicit set of assumptions about goals of rural seniors, and rural seniors hold another, it is not surprising that each group sees different needs for rural seniors. Health service needs are one place where the goals of the two groups may be at odds. While health-care planners might have a goal of providing hospital facilities within an hour's drive of most rural seniors, seniors' goals may be to live within a day's drive or an airplane flight of needed treatment. Similarly, while professionals might see provision of public transportation as a goal for rural small towns, residents of those towns may have as their goal a responsive, informal transportation system.

Clarifying whether an objective has been set by the professional or the rural senior allows us to address the philosophical question of who should determine whether there are unmet needs. Many of the needs assessments reviewed throughout this book suggest that rural seniors are often seen by professionals as underestimating their own needs.

Who, then, should determine what should be the goals of rural seniors? Some researchers have argued that seniors' evaluations of their environment are idiosyncratic and are less reflective of their actual need than of their personality (Windley and Scheidt, 1988). This perspective provides support for the argument that as objective outsiders, rural professionals are in the best position to determine goals and assess needs. As well, professionals have the advantage of broader perspectives on services from which to view relative need and service opportunities in a particular community. In contrast, the new ideology of health promotion supports the rights of seniors to determine their own destinies. If applied, this philosophy would surely encourage the provision of those services seen as necessary by seniors in the area. There is evidence that even the best services may not be used, if they have been developed without the expressed interest of potential clients. In one survey of seniors in Oxford county in Ontario, 97 percent said there were no disadvantages to living in the country. Most felt no need for, or interest in, Meals on Wheels, volunteer transportation or more information about the community (Brink, 1984). On the other hand, people frequently do not see a need for a service or seek information about a service until they have a critical need for it. Nonetheless, it seems that the new philosophies which encourage seniors to be independent and to take responsibility for their own quality of life, will lead to increasing emphasis on determining goals from the perspective of seniors themselves.

The second element of needs assessment, determination of the gap between the current situation and the goal, has also suffered from lack of sound methodology. Essential to a meaningful assessment of need is consistency in how needs are measured, since findings concerning level of need for services will vary depending upon the way a study is structured. Highest levels of needs are found when people are asked if they think a list of services is needed by others; when respondents in a study are known to be needing a service; or when service providers are asked about need (Connidis, 1985). Connidis argues that a more balanced approach to the assessment of need is to ask a representative sample of seniors whether they have used or are using any services; whether they need a service they are unable to find or afford; and which services are currently used or needed.

The needs of rural seniors can be understood as the gap between environmental demands and the competence of the older person in dealing with those demands (Lipish and Tindale, 1987). Environmental demands include the physical environment, including the characteristics of the neighbourhood and residence, and the personal environment, consisting of family, friends and neighbours. Individual competence is the ability of the individual to function, measured in terms of health, mobility and intellectual abilities. Asymmetry occurs when there is an imbalance between environmental demands and individual competence. An imbalance for rural seniors may be caused by such things as lack of supportive housing in the community, loss of spouse causing a move into town, or lack of resources to modify the existing environment if the individual does not want to relocate. Lipish and Tindale (1987) maintain that rural seniors make greater demands on the environment and have limited sources of social (especially formal) support.

Planning Service Delivery

Lipish and Tindale's comment that rural seniors have greater needs than do urban seniors is a conclusion, borne out by many of the findings reviewed in this book. Yet, as many others have pointed out, the rural elderly are not homogeneous. They vary in health and employment status, leisure patterns and income, quality of social networks and housing. They also vary in age by 30 or more years.

It is the heterogeneity of both rural seniors and rural areas that has made formal service delivery problematic. Awareness of this diversity has led to a rejection of urban service delivery models as appropriate to rural areas. Nonetheless, although there is considerable agreement that delivery of social services in small towns and rural communities should differ from that in urban areas (Coward, 1979), there is no consensus on how services can be developed to overcome some of the environmental exigencies of these areas. Rural areas often lack the necessary components to deliver housing and support services. It is costly to locate nursing homes in small communities or to deliver home care to a widely dispersed population. Similarly, it is difficult to construct and pay for seniors' housing in small communities (Brink, 1984).

Three promising approaches to developing more efficient and responsive service delivery systems are: developing program evaluation research on current and innovative service delivery models; determining the mix of formal and informal services; and using the rural culture to implement new services.

Program Evaluation Research

In addition to improved needs assessment research, there is a need for more research which evaluates the development and delivery of services to rural seniors (Coward and Cutler, 1989). Some of the fundamental changes occurring in rural communities make the monitoring of rural service delivery especially important. The influx of urban retirees into small towns and villages has added a group of people with urban experiences of service accessibility. These seniors may be more inclined to use a range of services at a distance rather than being limited to local resources. In contrast, farming communities in which women traditionally provided informal services to neighbours and family, now have high rates of off-farm employment. In these communities, increased levels of formal service delivery may be necessary to substitute for decreasing availability of informal help.

Financial crises faced by many resource-based rural communities have also affected their ability to expand or even maintain services for the elderly. Yet without documentation of changes in existing services or assessment of the adequacy of current services, it is difficult to know whether differences in service availability have a significant effect on the lives of seniors or their families.

In addition to the need to evaluate specific programs, our understanding of the implications of different structures and organizations of rural service networks needs to be expanded. Coward and Cutler (1989) argue that most rural services are like scaled-down urban services and rural service deliverers assume that the economies of scale make service delivery more expensive. However, research on the relative cost of urban versus rural service delivery has not been conducted, nor have evaluations been done on whether some ways of organizing service delivery are more efficient than others.

The Mix of Formal and Informal Services

Although Canadian rural areas have fewer organized services than do urban areas (National Advisory Council on Aging, 1986), strong informal networks in rural areas are seen to compensate for this discrepancy. A version of this argument exists in the urban literature as well, and has been challenged by Aronson (1985) who says that the assumption of the existence of an informal support system puts undue strain on women who are the major informal helpers. There is a risk that lack of formal support to rural seniors will be justified by policy makers on the grounds that informal help is more caring and responsive.

The issue of the ideal 'fit' in rural environments between informal and formal services has not been adequately addressed. In some rural communities such as Kaslo, the informal support system is well developed, since geographic isolation means that there are few existing formal services. However, even in such communities, newcomers may not have full access to informal support. In contrast, newly built retirement communities lack the history in which informal networks have developed. All communities need to determine what kinds of formal services are needed, how services can be successfully integrated with the existing informal support network to assist elderly residents to remain independent (Lipish and Tindale, 1987); and how the strain on informal helpers can be minimized (Connidis, 1985).

Implementing New Services in a Rural Community

The implementation of a new service may have a powerful impact on a small community. "A new agency is likely to cause a shift in the equilibrium, to force new patterns of interaction, and, finally, to achieve either integration into the system or extrusion from it" (Jeffrey and Reeve, 1978: 55). Similar to the entry process of new senior in-migrants, is the way new professionals enter an existing system which is relatively small, and in which people are well known to each other. The key to the acceptance of a new program by other professionals is a slow entry process of building ties with professionals already there. Those who are relocating from urban areas need to learn about the local culture and be in the community long enough to be seen as insiders. In a rural area, a person is seen as a useful professional only if he or she is also seen as trustworthy and is not believed to be a threat to the position of people already there (Jeffrey and Reeve, 1978).

The development and implementation of new services in rural communities has not received much attention from researchers. The perceived need for such services, the integration of new services into naturally occurring helping systems (Coward, 1979), and the ease of acceptance of new professionals into a community all warrant further study.

DEVELOPING SOCIAL POLICY FOR RURAL SENIORS

Each society makes decisions about its most pressing problems and the ideal solutions to those problems. Social policy is the formal way in which these problems are addressed. It is the organized effort of a society to deal with the identified needs of various groups within it (Jorgensen, 1989).

There has been a great deal of criticism aimed at the ways in which policy has been developed for the rural sector. The major concern is that rural social policy has been formed from an urban perspective that ignores the complexities of rural life. This urban emphasis is exemplified in a solution to problems of rural service delivery proposed by Tefertiller (1973). He suggested providing urban levels of services in both scope and quality, so that rural dwellers would be more satisfied with rural life and would not move to urban areas. The discussion in the previous section on assessment of service needs shows that even were this economically feasible, it would be difficult to establish that level of services in areas that are remote, that cannot attract professional service providers, or that consist of open countryside, with no centre from which to provide services.

Contemporary rural policy experts argue that "even today there is little evidence of a distinctly rural view or of orchestrated rural policies on planning issues affecting people and places in the open countryside" (Heenan, 1980: 45). Their concern is that the urban focus hinders the development of informed rural social policy, since the immense diversity of rural areas often goes unrecognized. The risk is that policy will be developed that is based on naïve notions that rural areas are simply more sparsely populated versions of urban areas. Rural areas differ from urban most importantly in their small population size and density, but also in terms of the distances between people and services. This results in a different "scale of life" for rural people which includes lack of employment options, less population diversity, more informal communication and regional governments run by the local power structure often to the detriment of the poor, minorities and the elderly (Watkins and Watkins, 1984).

How might this approach to rural policy development affect rural seniors? Because an urban bias is seen to mask the heterogeneity of rural areas, some groups of rural elders may be poorly served by traditional rural policy. People in remote rural areas are seldom assisted on a permanent basis by urban centred development, since such assistance is seen as too costly and inefficient (Fuller, 1984). Thus, native elders living in these areas may be subject to uneven levels of service provision. As well, any single rural area may be both a deprived and a desirable place to live (Watkins and Watkins, 1984). While Murray Nelson may be perfectly content with the few services that he knows in Kaslo, the Wilsons may soon be disillusioned by the lack of amenities to which they have become accustomed.

Steps in Policy Development for Rural Seniors

A shift in international perspectives on rural policy bodes well for more responsive policy development in Canada. A recent document published by the Organization for Economic Co-operation and Development (OECD, 1989) incorporates many of the issues that influence rural seniors. The thrust of the OECD document is that governments must redefine rural policy objectives, given the demographic, economic and socio-political trends in rural areas. The trends they recognize are central to issues of aging: increasing diversification of rural economies with the decline in agriculture; increasing heterogeneity of interests, values and lifestyles, with migration from urban to rural areas; the perceived importance of the cultural heritage of rural areas which needs to be protected; and the expansion of the cultural and economic horizons of many rural people beyond their communities to include regional, national and international perspectives. The OECD document identifies five steps in the policy development process. These can provide a framework for future planning in policy development for rural Canadian seniors.

The first step in policy development is problem identification which occurs when societal needs cannot be met through private action alone, when they are perceived as needs, and when they are placed on the public policy agenda. Fundamental to beginning the process of reform of rural policy for seniors is the question of how to get rural seniors issues onto the policy agenda. The call for a redefinition of rural policy, in conjunction with the emphasis on Canada's aging population, make this task seem more possible than it has in past decades. In rural areas, the phenomenon of small town Canada becoming a retirement haven, means that rural Canada now contains a cohort of relatively affluent, politically aware seniors, who are used to a style of life that requires the allocation of resources to communities in which they live. They are more likely to be vocal in their demands than are current residents for whom there has not been a dramatic change in lifestyle.

The emphasis on health promotion in Canada means that constituent groups like rural seniors will be encouraged to become more actively involved in developing their own communities to meet their needs. One way in which seniors have been encouraged to engage in policy development is through demonstration projects such as Project Involvement (Wolfe and Nutter, 1986). Project Involvement was carried out in three Alberta communities and involved the mobilization of seniors to discuss their concerns, feeding back those concerns to all seniors in the area, and forming action committees to act on those concerns. A limitation of this approach is the assumption that at all status levels, people can learn to be activists. This may be problematic for individuals who have few or no resources, or who have resources but lack the understanding of how to use them most effectively and efficiently. For many seniors, the concept of independent social action is still alien, and enormous tradeoffs are required for them to achieve even moderate success (Jorgensen, 1989).

The second step in policy development is policy formulation, the process of developing policy goals and strategies, and specific program initiatives to achieve those goals. Two challenges at this stage are to gain a clear understanding of socio-economic, environmental and political problems important in rural areas; and to develop feasible policy and program strategies for addressing rural problems effectively.

Many of the problems and assets of rural seniors in Canada have been discussed throughout this book. It is at the level of policy formulation that these are developed into specific action plans. There are many program initiatives that could be taken to provide support to rural seniors: income security, community integration, health promotion, housing, provision of leisure and recreational activities, and family counselling. Added to these are other issues that will have an impact on rural Canada. Environmental issues are of current importance and rural areas are now seen as the repository of ecological resources such as clean land, air and water which are important for the long-term needs of society. The development of policy goals for rural seniors requires a thorough understanding of issues raised by rural gerontologists, as well as by those in other fields such as political science and physical and human ecology. The state of our knowledge about rural seniors is very limited and so it is imperative that new research be conducted with policy implications in mind.

There is a range of strategies for policy development. One model of policy development which is consistent with the health promotion philosophy now popular in Canada, is seen in Ireland. Their idea is that rural development should reflect the ideas of and be the responsibility of local people. Policy development requires a partnership of community group representatives, local leaders and other individuals, who assume this responsibility for local development areas (OECD, 1989).

Step three is policy and program implementation. Putting rural programs into action requires a commitment of financial and human resources. This commitment requires various institutional partnership arrangements which may include different levels of government, government agencies, private business, professional associations, community voluntary organizations and other interests. The move toward integrated programs for Canadian seniors in general may have positive offshoots for rural seniors. One major effort in this area has been the provision of a single point of entry into health and social services. Program implementation also requires innovative approaches to service delivery to counteract the problem of low population density and the difficulty of attracting professionals to rural areas.

Step four is program evaluation. It includes both monitoring the performance of program initiatives and feeding the resulting information back into the previous stages of the public policymaking process. This is one of the weakest links in the rural policy development process. While there have been many needs assessments in rural Canada, rarely are subsequent programs followed up with comprehensive evaluations. Consequently, we know little about the success of programs. Not only are more comprehensive program evaluations required, program success must be determined from the perspective of the several constituencies who have different interests in the success of a program. While providers might look at economic feasibility or rates of use, clients or potential clients see a program as successful only if it meets some of their specific goals.

Because of the wide range of potential service needs of rural seniors, program evaluation needs to be done on a sector-specific basis. Thus, evaluations of health services in Kaslo would need to include assessments of the development, delivery and impact of health services for seniors in the area, including data on health status, perceived health needs (from the perspective of seniors and health professionals), perceived adequacy and accessibility of services. Evaluation of recreational services or income security programs require separate initiatives.

Although the diversity of rural elders is apparent, many services tend to be targeted to groups of "frail" seniors (Windley and Scheidt, 1988). This may be an appropriate emphasis since most seniors manage without the aid of formal services (Connidis, 1985). However, targeting a small group of rural seniors may mean that rural social policies are too narrowly focused. At the policy development stage at least, all rural seniors must be considered.

The final step is policy and program termination which includes the elimination of public policies and programs that are ineffective or no longer useful or feasible (OECD, 1989). When sound policy development has been undertaken, this step should follow logically, since there are data on effectiveness and timeliness of programs. However, services also have unintended outcomes: people who have provided them are friends, service centres become social centres. Effectiveness of programs may need to include both intended and unintended outcomes.

Prevailing social policy has a profound effect on the lives of the people living under that policy, since social policies set out principles and courses of action. "They regulate the development, allocation, and distribution of statuses and roles and their accompanying constraints, rewards, and entitlements among individuals and social units in a society, and they determine the distribution of resources and shape the quality of life" (Jorgensen, 1989: 291). As the nature of rural Canada continues to change, informed social policy developed with seniors in mind can have a positive effect on their experiences of aging.

BIBLIOGRAPHY

Adams, D.
    1975   "Who Are the Rural Aged?" In R. C. Atchley (ed.). *Rural Environments and Aging*. Washington: Gerontological Society of America. 11-21.

Agbayewa, M. O., and B. Michalski
    1984   "Accommodation Preference in the Senior Years." *Canadian Journal of Public Health* 75:176-179.

Alberta, Province of
    1988   "A New Vision for Long Term Care: Meeting the Need." The Committee on Long Term Care for Senior Citizens. D. Mirosh, Chair.

Alberta Agriculture
    1988   *Strengthening Rural Alberta*. Edmonton, Alberta: Government of Alberta

Alberta Committee on Long Term Care for Senior Citizens
    1988   *A New Vision for Long Term Care: Meeting the Need*. Edmonton, Alberta: Queen's Printer for Alberta.

Alberta Indian Health Care Commission
    1984   *NNADAP Needs Assessment Report*. Edmonton, Alberta: Government of Alberta.
    no date *Objectives of the Commission*. Edmonton, Alberta: Government of Alberta.

Alberta Long Term Care Institutions Branch
    1989   *Values and Principles to Guide the Development of a Coordinated Institutional Long Term Care System in Alberta*. Edmonton, Alberta: Government of Alberta.

Alberta Recreation and Parks
    1984a   *A Look at Leisure #18: Recreation Patterns of Older Adults*. Edmonton, Alberta: Government of Alberta.
    1984b   *A Look at Leisure #19: Community Type Variations in Recreation Patterns*. Edmonton, Alberta. Government of Alberta.
    1988   *1988 General Recreation Survey*. Edmonton, Alberta: Government of Alberta.

Alberta Senior Citizens' Secretariat
  1986   *The Preventive Approach, Preventive Programs and Alberta's Seniors.*
          Edmonton, Alberta: Government of Alberta.
Arcury, T.
  1984   "Household Composition and Economic Change in a Rural
          Community, 1900-1980: Testing Two Models." *American Eth-
          nologist* 11: 677-698.
  1986   "Rural Elderly Household Life-course Transitions, 1900 and
          1980 Compared." *Journal of Family History* 11(1): 55-76.
Armstrong, M. B., and A. Fuller
  1979   "Transportation in the Countryside: An Ontario Case Study."
          Paper presented to the Annual Meeting of the Canadian Asso-
          ciation of Geographers, Victoria, British Columbia, May.
Aronson, J.
  1985   "Family Care of the Elderly: Underlying Assumptions and their
          Consequences." *Canadian Journal on Aging* 4(3): 115-126.
Atchley, R.
  1983   *Aging: Continuity and Change.* Belmont, California: Wadsworth.
Atchley, R., and T. O. Byerts (eds.)
  1975   *Rural Environments and Aging.* Washington, D.C.: Department
          of Health, Education, and Welfare.
Bauder, W., and J. Doerflinger
  1967   "Work Roles Among the Rural Aged." In E. Youmans (ed.).
          Older Rural Americans: A Sociological Perspective. Lexington:
          University of Kentucky Press. 22-43.
Beland, F.
  1986   "Patterns of Health and Social Service Utilization." Paper pre-
          sented to the Annual Meeting of the Canadian Association on
          Gerontology, Quebec City, Quebec.
Bengston, V.
  1971   "Generational Difference and the Developmental Stake." *Aging
          and Human Development.* 2: 249-260.
Berry, B. A. and A. E. Davis
  1978   "Community Mental Health Ideology: A Problematic Model for
          Rural Areas." *American Journal of Orthopsychiatry* 48(4): 673-679.
Bienvenue, R., and B. Havens
  1986   "Structural Inequalities, Informal Networks: A Comparison of Native
          and Non-native Elderly." *Canadian Journal on Aging* 5(4): 241-248.
Bilby, R. W., and R. Benson
  1977   "Public Perceptions of Rural County Social Service Agencies."
          Journal of Sociology and Social Welfare 47: 1033-1054.
Black, M.
  1985   "Health and Social Support of Older Adults in the Community."
          Canadian Journal on Aging 4(4): 213-226.

Blackburn, D. J.
  1987 "Canada's Prairie Provinces." *The Rural Sociologist* 75: 410-420.
Blair, D. I.
  1981 "Use of Formal and Informal Support Resources by Elderly in a Rural Community." Unpublished Master's thesis, University of Calgary.
Bobet, E.
  1989 "Indian Mortality." *Canadian Social Trends* 15: 11-14.
Bond, J. B.
  1986 "Aging: A Cultural Perspective." Keynote address to the annual meeting of the Alberta Association on Gerontology, Lake Louise, Alberta, May.
Bond, J. B. and C. Harvey
  1987 "Familial Support of the Elderly in a Rural Mennonite Community." *Canadian Journal on Aging* 6(1): 7-17.
Boss, P.
  1986 "Farm Family Displacement and Stress." In Farm Foundation (ed.). *Increasing Understanding of Public Problems and Policies —1985*. Oakbrook, Ill: Farm Foundation. 61-78.
Bouquet, M.
  1982 "Production and Reproduction of Family Farms in South-West England." *Sociologica Ruralis* 20: 227-244.
Brandenburg, J., W. Greiner, E. Hamilton-Smith, H. Scholten, R. Senior, and J. Webb
  1982 "A Conceptual Model of How People Adopt Recreation Activities." *Leisure Studies* 1: 263-276.
Break, H.
  1985 "Impact Study of the Sandy Cove Acres Retirement Community on Existing Home Care/Support Services in Innisfil Township." Unpublished Master's thesis, Department of Rural Planning and Development, University of Guelph.
Brillon, Y.
  1987 *Victimization and Fear of Crime among the Elderly.* Toronto: Butterworths.
Brink, S.
  1984 "Housing Elderly People in Canada." Paper presented to the annual meeting of the Canadian Association on Gerontology, Vancouver, British Columbia.
Brown, K. H., and A. Martin Matthews
  1981 "Changes in the Welfare of the Recently Retired: Rural-Urban Comparisons." Paper presented to the annual meeting of the Rural Sociological Society, Guelph, Ontario, August.
Bureau of Statistics
  1893 "Occupations Census of Canada 1890-91." Vol. 2, Table xii. Ottawa: E. Dawson.

Butler, R. W.
   1984   "The Impact of Informal Recreation on Rural Canada." In M.
           Bunce and M. Troughton (eds.). *The Pressure of Change in Rural
           Canada.* Downsview, Ontario: York University, Geographical
           Monograph No. 14. Pp. 216-240.
Canada
   1982   Canadian Governmental Report on Aging. Ottawa: Minister of
           Supply and Services Canada.
The Canadian Encyclopaedia
   1985   1st ed. Edmonton Alberta: Hurtig Publishers.
Cape, E.
   1984   "The Distaff Side of Retiring to the Country." Paper presented
           to the Annual Meeting of the Canadian Sociology and Anthro-
           pology Association, Guelph, Ontario, June.
   1982   "Aging Women in Rural Society: Out of Sight, Out of Mind."
           Resources for Feminist Research 11: 214-215.
Chamberlain, S.
   1976   "Study of the Housing and Health Care Needs of the Elderly
           Persons of North Frontenac." School of Social Work, Carleton
           University.
Connidis, I.
   1985   "The Service Needs of Older People: Implications for Public
           Policy." *Canadian Journal on Aging* 4(1): 3-9.
   1987   "Life in Old Age: The View from the Top." In V. Marshall (ed.).
           Aging in Canada: Social Perspectives. Second Edition. Markham,
           Fitzhenry and Whiteside. Pp. 451-472.
   1989   *Family Ties and Aging:* Toronto: Butterworths.
Connidis, I. and J. Rempel
   1983   "The Living Arrangements of Older Residents: The Role of
           Gender, Marital Status, Age, and Family Size." *Canadian Journal
           on Aging* 2(3): 91-105.
Cook, A. K.
   1987   "Nonmetropolitan Migration: The Influence of Neglected
           Variables." *Rural Sociology* 52(3): 409-418.
Corin, E.
   1984   "Manières de Vivre, Manières de Dire: Réseau Social et Sociabilité
           Quotidienne des Personnes au Québec." *Questions de Culture* 6:
           157-186.
Corin, E., J. Tremblay, T. Sherif, and L. Bergeron
   1984   "Entre les Services Professionnels et les Réseaux Sociaux: les
           Stratégies d'existence des Personnes Agées." *Sociologie et Sociétés*
           16(2): 89-104.
Costello, T. P., R. C. Pugh, B. Steadman, and R. A. Kane
   1977   "Perceptions of Urban Versus Rural Hospital Patients About

Return to their Communities." *Journal of the American Geriatrics Society* 25: 552-555.

Coward, R. T.
1979   "Planning Community Services for the Rural Elderly: Implications from Research." *The Gerontologist* 19(3): 275-282.

Coward, R. T. and S. J. Cutler
1988   "The Concept of a Continuum of Residence: Comparing Activities of Daily Living Among the Elderly." *Journal of Rural Studies* 4(2): 159-168.
1989   "Informal and Formal Health Care Systems for the Rural Elderly." *Health Services Research* 23(6): 785-806.

Coward, R. T., S. Cutler, and F. Schmidt
1988   "Differences in the Household Composition of Elders by Age, Gender and Residence." Paper presented to the Annual Meeting of the National Council on Family Relations, Philadelphia, Pennsylvania.

Cunningham, D., P. A. Rechnitzer, and A. P. Donner
1986   "Exercise Training and the Speed of Self-selected Walking Pace in Men at Retirement." *Canadian Journal on Aging* 5(1): 19-26.

Davis, D. L.
1985   Belligerent Legends: Bickering and Feuding Among Outport Octogenarians. *Aging and Society* 5: 431-448.

Deimling, G., and L. Huber
1981   "The Availability and Participation of Immediate Kin in Caring for Rural Elderly." Paper presented to the annual meeting of the Gerontological Society of America, Toronto, Ontario.

Department of Health and Department of Social Services, Government of the Northwest Territories
1987   *Aged, Disabled and Chronically Ill: 1985/86 Assessment Project.* Yellowknife, Northwest Territories.

Dorfman, L. and A. Heckert
1988   "Egalitarianism in Retired Rural Couples: Household Tasks, Decision-making and Leisure Activities." *Family Relations* 37: 73-78.

Dorfman, L., D. Heckert, E. Hill, and F. Kohout
1988   "Retirement Satisfaction in Rural Husbands and Wives." *Rural Sociology 53(1): 25-39.*

Dorfman, L. and E. Hill
1986   "Rural Housewives and Retirement: Joint Decision-making Matters." *Family Relations.* 35: 507-514.

Doucette, L.
1987   "Aging in the Context of Regional Culture: A Study of Late-life Creativity." Paper presented to the annual meeting of the Canadian Association on Gerontology, Calgary, Alberta, October.

Earle, V.
1984   "Report of a Study to Develop a Comprehensive Proposal for a
         Pilot Caregiver Relief Program." Durham Region Community
         Care Association, Durham, Ontario.
Epp, J.
1986   *Achieving Health for All: A Framework for Health Promotion.* Ot-
         tawa: Health and Welfare Canada.
Fiaz , N.
1983   *Senior Citizens in Antigonish County: Current Issues.* Antigonish, Nova
         Scotia: Extension Department, St. Francis Xavier University.
Fisher, A. D.
1986   "Great Plains Ethnology." In R. Morrison and C. R. Wilson
         (eds.). *Native Peoples: The Canadian Experience.* Toronto:
         McClelland and Stewart. Pp. 358-374.
Flaskerud, J. H. and F. J. Kuiz
1984   "Determining the Need for Mental Health Services in Rural
         Areas." *American Journal of Community Psychology* 12: 497-510.
Flynn, D.
1987   "Rural Life in Canada: Surviving the Empty Northland and the
         American River Presence." *The Rural Sociologist* 75: 388-394.
Fritz, E., and S. Orlowski
1983   *An Exploratory Study of Homebound, Rural Elderly.* Guelph, Ontario.
         Department of Consumer Studies, University of Guelph.
Fuller, A.
1984   "Forging New Links for Rural Development and Planning in
         Canada." In M. Bunce and M. Troughton (eds.). *The Pressure of
         Change in Rural Canada.* Downsview, Ontario: York University,
         Geographical Monograph No. 14. Pp. 216-240.
Gasson, R.
1984   "Farm Women in Europe: Their Need for Off-Farm Employ-
         ment." *Sociologia Ruralis* 24(3/4): 216-227.
Gennaro, G.
1983   "The Elderly and Rural Society: The Results of a Research
         Survey." *Sociologia* 17(3): 125-153.
Gillis, D.
1987   "Indicators of Health among Elderly Native Canadians." Paper
         presented to the annual meeting of the Canadian Association on
         Gerontology, Calgary, Alberta.
Goodstadt, M., R. Simpson, and P. Loranger
1987   "Health Promotion: A Conceptual Integration." *American
         Journal of Health Promotion.* 1(3): 58-63.
Grant, P. R. and B. Rice
1983   "Transportation Problems of the Rural Elderly." *Canadian
         Journal on Aging.* 2: 107-124.

Grudinzki, E., and E. Passmore
1988   *Making it in Tough Times: A Research Report on the Continuity of the Farm Business in Times of Economic Downturn.* Edmonton, Alberta: Alberta Agriculture, Region Three.
Guemple, L.
1980   "Growing Old in Inuit Society." In V. Marshall (ed.). *Aging in Canada: Social Perspectives.* Don Mills, Ontario: Fitzhenry and Whiteside. Pp. 95-101.
Gunn, J., J. Verkley, and L. Newman
1983   *Older Canadian Homeowners: A Literature Review.* Ottawa, Ontario: Canada Mortgage and Housing Corporation.
Hammersley, M. and P. Atkinson
1983   *Ethnography: Principles in Practice.* London: Tavistock Publications.
Harbert, A. S., and C. W. Wilkinson
1979   "Growing Old in Rural America." *Aging* 291: 36-40.
Harper, S.
1987   "The Kinship Network of the Rural Aged: A Comparison of the Indigenous Elderly and the Retired Inmigrant." *Ageing and Society* 7: 303-327.
Havens, B.
1980   "Differentiation of Unmet Needs Using Analysis by Age/sex Cohorts." In V. Marshall (ed.). *Aging in Canada: Social Perspectives.* Don Mills, Ontario: Fitzhenry and Whiteside. Pp. 215-221
Health and Welfare Canada
1981   *The Health of Canadians: A Report of the Canada Health Survey.* Ottawa, Ontario. Minister of Supply and Services.
1989   *Active Health Report on Seniors.* Ottawa, Ontario. Minister of Supply and Services.
Health and Welfare Canada. Health Promotion Directorate
1984   *Nutrition Promotion with Seniors: A Guide for Those who Work with Seniors.* Ottawa: Minister of Supply and Services.
Heenan, L.
1980   "Contemporary New Zealand Rural Population Trends. Planning Issues, Response and Challenge." *New Zealand Agricultural Science* 14(1), 45-55.
Hiltner, J., B. Smith, and J. A. Sullivan
1986   "The Utilization of Social and Recreational Services by the Elderly: A Case Study of Northwestern Ohio." *Economic Geography* 62(3): 232-240.
Hodge, G.
1984   *Shelter and Services for the Small Town Elderly: The Role of Assisted Housing.* Ottawa: Canada Mortgage and Housing Corporation.
Hodge, G., and J. B. Collins
1987   *The Elderly in Canada's Small Towns.* Vancouver, British Co-

lumbia: The Centre for Human Settlements, University of British Columbia.

Hohn, N.
1986   *Issues Affecting Older Natives in Alberta.* Edmonton, Alberta: Alberta Senior Citizens Secretariat.

Humboldt Community Survey Committee.
1976   *Humboldt Community Survey.* Humboldt, Saskatchewan.

Hunt, M., A. Feldt, A. Marans, L. Pastalan, and K. Vakalo
1984   *Retirement Communities: An American Original.* New York: The Haworth Press.

Hunt, S., and A. Weiner
1982   "Relationships Between Meanings of Work and Meanings of Leisure in a Retirement Community." *Recreation Research Review* 9(2): 29-37.

Jeffrey, M. and R. Reeve
1978   "Community Mental Health Services in Rural Areas: Some Practical Issues." *Community Mental Health Journal* 14(1): 54-62.

Johnson, C., and F. Johnson
1983   "A Micro-Analysis of Senility: The Responses of the Family and the Health Professionals." *Culture, Medicine and Psychiatry.* 7: 77-96.

Johnson, C. L. and D. J. Catalano
1983   "A Longitudinal Study of Family Supports to Impaired Elderly." *The Gerontologist* 23, 612-618.

Jorgensen, L. A.
1989   "Women and Aging: Perspectives on Public and Social Policy". In J. D. Garner, and S. O. Mercer (eds.). *Women as They Age: Challenge, Opportunity, and Triumph.* New York: The Haworth Press. Pp. 291-316.

Joseph, A., and A. Fuller
1988   "Aging in Rural Communities: Interrelated Issues in Housing, Services and Transportation." Papers in Rural Aging, University of Guelph, Guelph, Ontario.

Keating, N.
1987   "Reducing Stress of Farm Men and Women." *Family Relations* 36: 358-363.
1989   "The Role of the Family in Long Term Care." Plenary presentation to the annual meeting of the Health Unit Association of Alberta and the Alberta Hospital Association, Calgary, Alberta.

Keating, N., and G. Brundin
1983   "Factors in Consideration of Moving by Older Rural Men." *Canadian Home Economics Journal,* 33(3): 137-140.

Keating, N., M. Doherty, and B. Munro
1987   "The Whole Economy: Resource Allocation of Alberta Farm

Women and Men." *Canadian Home Economics Journal* 37(3): 135-139.

Keating, N., and J. Marshall
1980   "The Process of Retirement: the Rural Self-Employed." *The Gerontologist* 20(4): 437-443.

Keating, N., and B. Munro
1988   "Farm Women, Farm Work." *Sex Roles* 19(3/4): 155-168.
1989   "Transferring the Family Farm: Process and Implications." *Family Relations* 38: 215-218.

Keith, P., and A. Nauta
1988   "Old and Single in the City and in the Country: Activities of the Unmarried." *Family Relations* 37: 79-83.

Kent County District Health Council
1983   *Long Term Care Study.* Chatham, Ontario.

Kivett, V. R.
1985   "Aging in Rural Society: Non-Kin Community Relations and Participation." In R. Coward and G. Lee (eds.). *The Elderly in Rural Society*, New York: Springer. Pp. 171-191.
1988a   "Aging in a Rural Place: The Elusive Source of Well-Being." *Journal of Rural Studies* 4(2): 125-132.
1988b   "Older Rural Fathers and Sons: Patterns of Association and Helping." *Family Relations* 37: 62-67.

Kivett, V. R., and R. Learner
1980   "Situational Influences on the Morale of Older Rural Adults in Child Shared Households." Paper presented to the annual meeting of the Gerontological Society, San Diego, California, November.

Kluckhohn, F. R.
1958   "Variations in the Basic Values of Family Systems." *Social Casework* 39:63-72.

Kozma, A., and M. J. Stones
1983   "Predictors of Happiness." *Journal of Gerontology* 38: 626-628.

Krout, J. A.
1988   "The Elderly in Rural Environments." *Journal of Rural Studies* 4(2): 103-114.

Leacy, F. H. (ed.)
1983   *Historical Statistics of Canada.* 2nd ed. Ottawa: Minister of Supply and Services.

Lee, J.
1987   "Women as Non-family Farmworkers." In Canadian Advisory Council on the Status of Women (eds.). *Growing Strong: Women in Agriculture.* Ottawa: Canadian Advisory Council on the Status of Women. Pp. 91-122.

Little, J.
  1986   "Feminist Perspectives in Rural Geography: An Introduction."
          Journal of Rural Studies 2: 1-8.
Lipish, A., and J. A. Tindale
  1987   "Competence and Environmental Press in a Rural Setting." Paper
          presented to the annual meeting of the Canadian Association on
          Gerontology, Calgary, Alberta.
Lubben, J., P. Weiler, I. Chi, and F. DeJong
  1988   "Health Promotion for the Rural Elderly." *The Journal of Rural
          Health* 4(3): 85-96.
Maclouf, P., and A. Lion
  1983   "Aging in Remote Rural Areas: A Challenge to Social and
          Medical Services." *Eurosocial* 24. Vienna: European Centre for
          Social Welfare Training and Research.
Mark, S.
  1981   *Community Dialogue on the Needs of the Elderly in Lanark, Leeds and
          Grenville.* Lanark, Ontario: Leeds and Grenville District Health
          Council.
Martin Matthews, A.
  1988a   "Aging in Rural Canada." In E. Rathbone-McCuan and B. Havens
          (eds.). *North American Elders: United States and Canadian Perspectives.*
          Westport, Connecticut: Greenwood Press. Pp. 143-160.
  1988b   "Variations in the Conceptualization and Measurement of Ru-
          rality: Conflicting Findings on the Elderly Widowed." *Journal of
          Rural Studies* 4(2): 141-150.
Martin Matthews, A., K. Brown, C. Davis, and M. Denton
  1982   "A Crisis Assessment Technique for the Evaluation of Life
          Events: Transition to Retirement as an Example." *Canadian
          Journal on Aging* 1(3/4): 28-39.
Martin Matthews, A., and A. Vanden Heuvel
  1986   "Conceptual and Methodological Issues in Research on Aging in Rural
          versus Urban Environments." *Canadian Journal on Aging* 5:49-60.
Matthews, R.
  1983   *The Creation of Regional Dependency.* Toronto: University of Toronto
          Press.
McCay, B.
  1987   "Old People and Social Relations in a Newfoundland 'Outport'."
          In H. Strange and M. Teitelbaum (eds.).   *Aging and Cultural
          Diversity.* South Hadley, Mass.: Bergen and Garvey. Pp. 61-87.
McClelland, N. and C. Miles
  1987   *1985/1986 Assessment Project: Aged, Disabled and Chronically Ill.*
          Yellowknife, NWT: Department of Social Services and Health,
          Government of the Northwest Territories.

McDonald, L., and R. Wanner
1982   "Work Past Age 65 in Canada: A Socioeconomic Analysis."
        Aging and Work 5: 169-180.
1989   *Retirement in Canada.* Toronto: Butterworths.
McGhee, J.
1985   "The Effects of Siblings on the Life Satisfaction of the Rural
        Elderly." *Journal of Marriage and the Family* 47: 85-91.
McNeil, K., A. Kozma, M. Stones, and E. Hannah
1986   "Measurement of Psychological Hardiness in Older Adults."
        Canadian Journal on Aging 5(1): 43-48.
McPherson, B. D.
1978   "Aging and Involvement in Physical Activity: A Sociological
        Perspective." In F. Landry and W. Orban (eds.). *Physical Activity
        and Human Well-being.* Miami, Florida: Symposia Specialists.
        Pp. 11-125.
1986   "Sport, Health, Well-being and Aging: Some Conceptual and
        Methodological Issues and Questions for Sport Scientists." In
        B. D. McPherson (ed.). *Sport and Aging.* Champaign, Illinois:
        Human Kinetics Press. Pp. 3-23.
1988   "Aging with Excellence: The Contribution of Physical Activity to
        Health and Wellness." In L. McDonald and N. Keating (eds.).
        Canadian Gerontological Collection VI: Aging with Excellence.
        Calgary, Alberta: Canadian Association on Gerontology. Pp.
        91-124.
1990   *Aging as a Social Process: An Introduction to Individual and Popula-
        tion Aging.* 2nd ed. Toronto, Ontario: Butterworths. Pp. 421-450.
McPherson, B. D., and C. A. Kozlik
1987   "Age Patterns in Leisure Participation: The Canadian Case." In
        V. Marshall (ed.). *Aging in Canada: Social Perspectives.* Markham,
        Ontario: Fitzhenry and Whiteside. Pp. 211-227.
Mercier, J., L. Paulson, and E. Morris
1988   "Rural and Urban Elderly: Differences in the Quality of the
        Parent-Child Relationship. *Family Relations* 37: 68-72.
Michalos, A. C.
1982   "The Satisfaction and Happiness of Some Senior Citizens in
        Rural Ontario." *Social Indicators Research* 11: 1-30.
Michalos, A., A. Fuller, J. Mage, A. Martin Matthews, and L. Wood.
1980   "Towards an Understanding of the Rural Elderly." Toronto,
        Ontario: Ontario Advisory Council on Senior Citizens.
Miller, M. K., and A. E. Luloff
1981   "Who is Rural? A Typological Approach to the Examination of
        Rurality." *Rural Sociology* 46: 608-625.

Mobily, K., D. Leslie, J. Lemke, R. Wallace, and F. Kohout
   1987   "Leisure Patterns and Attitudes of the Rural Elderly." *The Journal of Applied Gerontology* 5(2): 201-214.
Moore, C. D., and S. Pfeiffer
   1987   "A Cross-Longitudinal Study of Physical Fitness in Ontario Dairy Farmers Aged Fifty Years and Over." *Canadian Journal on Aging* 6(3): 189-198.
Morris, J., and S. Sherwood
   1984   "Informal Support Resources for Vulnerable Elderly Persons: Can They be Counted on, Why do They Work?" *International Journal on Aging and Human Development* 18(2): 81-98.
Morton, M., S. Polowin, C. Murphy, and A. McDonald
   1984   "Survey of Needs of Seniors in the Township of Rideau." Rideau, Ontario: Township of Rideau Senior Citizens' Service Centre.
National Advisory Council on Aging
   1981   *Priorities for Action.* Ottawa: Minister of Supply and Services.
   1983   *Moving Ahead with Aging in Canada.* Ottawa: Minister of Supply and Services.
   1986   "Toward a Community Support Policy for Canadians." Ottawa, Ontario: Minister of Supply and Services.
Neerlandia Historical Society
   1985   *A Furrow Laid Bare.* Neerlandia Historical Society, Neerlandia, Alberta.
Nelson, G. M.
   1983   "A Comparison of Title XX Services to the Urban and Rural Elderly." *Journal of Gerontological Social Work* 6: 3-23.
Neufeldt, A. H.
   1974   *Mennonite Central Committee Commission on Aging.* Mennonite Central Committee of Saskatchewan.
Newby, H.
   1986   "Locality and Rurality: The Restructuring of Rural Social Relations." *Regional Studies* 20: 209-215.
Newhouse, J. and W. McAuley
   1987   "Use of Informal In-Home Care by Rural Elders." *Family Relations* 36: 456-460.
Northcott, H. C.
   1984   "The Interprovincial Migration of Canada's Elderly: 1956-61 and 1971-76." *Canadian Journal on Aging* 3: 3-22.
Novak, M.
   1985   *Successful Aging: The Myths, Realities and Future of Aging in Canada.* Markham, Ontario: Penguin Books.
Office for Senior Citizens' Affairs
   1986   *A New Agenda: Health and Social Service Strategies for Ontario's Seniors.* Toronto: Queen's Printer.

Olinek, B.
1989   "Respite Care Services: Rationale, Design, and Evaluation." MSc Paper, University of Alberta, Edmonton, Alberta.
O'Neil, J.
1987   "Health Care in a Central Canadian Arctic Community: Continuities and Change." In D. Coburn, C. D'Arcy, G. Torrance and P. New (eds.). *Health and Canadian Society: Sociological Perspectives.* Markham, Ontario: Fitzhenry and Whiteside. Pp 141-158.
Ontario Advisory Council for Disabled Persons.
1988   *Independent Living: The Time is Now.* Toronto: Government of Ontario.
Ontario Advisory Council on Senior Citizens
1980   *Towards an Understanding of the Rural Elderly.* Toronto.
Ontario Ministry of Municipal Affairs
1985   *Retirement Communities.* Toronto: Government of Ontario.
Organization for Economic Co-operation and Development (OECD)
1989   *Partnerships for Rural Development.* Paris: OECD Technical Co-operation Service.
Ouelette, P.
1986   "The Leisure Participation and Enjoyment Patterns of French and English Speaking Members of Senior Citizen's Clubs in New Brunswick, Canada." *Canadian Journal on Aging* 5(4): 257-268.
Palmore, E.
1983   "Health Care Needs of the Rural Elderly." *International Journal of Aging and Human Development* 18(1): 39-45.
Ponting, J. R.
1986   "Assessing a Generation of Change." In J. R. Ponting (ed.). *Arduous Journey: Canadian Indians and Decolonization.* Toronto, Ontario: McCelland and Stewart. Pp. 394-409.
Preston, D. B. and P. K. Mansfield
1984   "An Exploration of Stressful Life Events, Illness and Coping Among the Rural Elderly." *The Gerontologist* 24(5): 490-494.
Quebec Ministry of Social Services
1985   *Sharing a New Age: Policy of the Ministry of Social Affairs in Regard to Elderly Persons.* Quebec: Government of Quebec.
Raiwet, C.
1989   "As Long as we Have Our Health: The Experience of Age-Related Physical Change for Rural Elderly Couples." MSc Thesis. University of Alberta, Edmonton, Alberta.
Recker, G.T. and P.T. Wong
1984   "Psychological and Physical Well-being in the Elderly: The Perceived Well-being Scale (PWB). *Canadian Journal on Aging* 3(1): 23-32.

Regional Steering Committee for Geriatric Services in the North Peace River
        Region
    1986   A New Beginning: A Review of the Needs of Seniors in the Peace
            River Health Unit, Peace River, Alberta.
Reinharz, S., and G. Rowles
    1988   *Qualitative Gerontology*. New York: Springer.
Roling, N.
    1987   *Whither Rural Extension?* Guelph, Ontario: Department of Rural
            Extension Studies, University of Guelph.
Ross, H. M.
    1984   Concepts of Good Health Held by Rural Elders in Eastern
            Canada." Paper presented to the annual meeting of the Cana-
            dian Association on Gerontology, Vancouver, British Columbia.
Rowe, G. and M. Norris
    1985   "Mortality Projections of Registered Indians, 1982 to 1986."
            Ottawa: Minister of Indian Affairs and Northern Development.
Rowles, G. D.
    1983   "Between Worlds: A Relocation Dilemma for the Appalachian
            Elderly." *International Journal of Aging and Human Development*
            17: 301-314.
    1986   "The Rural Elderly and the Church." *Journal of Religion and Aging*
            2: 79-98.
    1988   "What's Rural about Rural Aging? An Appalachian Perspec-
            tive." *Journal of Rural Studies* 4(2): 115-124.
Santerre, R.
    1982   "Masculinité et Vieillissement dans le Bas-Saint-Laurent: Notes
            de Recherche." *Anthropologie et Sociétés* 63: 115-128.
Scheidt, R. J.
    1984   "A Taxonomy of Well-Being for Small-Town Elderly: A Case for
            Rural Diversity." *The Gerontologist* 24(1): 84-90.
Scott, J., and V. Kivett
    1980   "The Widowed, Black, Older Adult in the Rural South: Impli-
            cations for Policy." *Family Relations* 29(1): 83-90.
Scott, J. P., and K. Roberto
    1987   "Informal Supports of Older Adults : A Rural-Urban Compari-
            son." *Family Relations* 36: 444-449.
Selles, R.
    1988   "Retirement Among Dutch-Canadian Farmers." Unpublished
            MSc thesis, University of Alberta, Edmonton, Alberta.
Selles, R. and N. Keating
    1989   "La Transmission des Fermes par les Albertainages d'origine
            Hollandaise." In R. Santerre and D. Meintel (eds.). *Veiller au
            Québec, en Afrique et Ailleurs*. Laval, University of Laval Press.

Senior Citizens Provincial Council.
1983   *Profile '83 — the Senior Population in Saskatchewan* (Vols. 1-4). Regina, SK: Senior Citizens Provincial Council.
1987   *A Survey of the Transportation Patterns and Needs of the Urban Elderly in Saskatchewan.* Regina, Saskatchewan: Senior Citizens Provincial Council.
Senior Citizens Research Committee
1980   *Property Taxes and other Problems of the Elderly in Nova Scotia.* Halifax, NS: Regional and Urban Studies Centre, Dalhousie University.
Shamir, B., and H. Ruskin
1983   "Type of Community as a Moderator of Work-leisure Relationships: A Comparative Study of Kibbutz Residents and Urban Residents." *Journal of Occupational Behavior* 4: 209-221.
Shapiro, E.
1985   "Caring about Carers: What have We Learned from Research and Experience?" Keynote address to the Alberta Association on Gerontology, Lake Louise, Alberta.
Shapiro, E. and L. Roos
(1984)   "Using Health Care: Rural/Urban Differences Among the Manitoba Elderly." *The Gerontologist* 24(3), 270-274.
Sharpe, T., M. Smith, and A. Barbre
1985   "Medicine Use Among the Rural Elderly." *Journal of Health and Social Behavior* 26: 113-127.
Shenk, D. and D. McTavish
1988   "Aging Women In Minnesota: Rural-Non-Rural Differences in Life-History Text." *Journal of Rural Studies* 4(2):133-140.
Snell, L. M., and K. Brown
1987   "Financial Strategies of the Recently Retired." *Canadian Journal on Aging* 6(4): 290-303.
Sofranko, A., Fliegel, F. and N. Glasgow
1983   "Older Urban Migrants in Rural Settings: Problems and Prospects." *International Journal of Aging and Human Development* 16:297-309.
Stafford, J.
1984   "Constraints on Out-migration of Retirees in Isolated Towns." Paper presented to the annual meeting of the Blue Collar Conference, Toronto, Ontario, May.
Staines, G. L.
1980   "Spillover Versus Compensation: A Review of the Literature on the Relationship between Work and Nonwork." *Human Relations* 33(2): 111-129.
Stalwick, H.
1983   "Canadian Perspective on Aging in Remote Rural Areas: A Challenge

for Socio-medical Services." Paper presented to the International Expert Group Meeting on Aging in Remote Areas, Limoges, France.

Statistics Canada
1982   *Canadian Government Report on Aging.* Ottawa: Minister of Supply and Services Canada.

1982   *Population: Population by Marital Status and Sex. 1981 Census.* (Catalogue #92-901, Table 7). Ottawa: Minister of Supply and Services Canada.

1984a   *Population Labour Force — Occupation By Demographic and Educational Characteristics 1981* (Catalogue #92-917). Ottawa: Minister of Supply and Services Canada.

1984b   *Occupied Private Dwellings, 1981 Census of Canada.* (Catalogue #92-932 Table 7). Ottawa: Minister of Supply and Services Canada.

1984c   *Population Labour Force Activity* (Catalogue #92-915), Ottawa: Minister of Supply and Services Canada.

1987a   *Census Canada 1986 Reference Dictionary.* (Catalogue #99-101E). Ottawa, Ontario: Minister of Supply and Services Canada.

1987b   *The Nation: Age, Sex and Marital Status.* (Catalogue #93-101) Ottawa: Minister of Supply and Services Canada.

1988   *Canada's Seniors: A Dynamic Force.* Ottawa: Minister of Supply and Services Canada.

1988a   *Profiles British Columbia, Part 2: Census Divisions and Subdivisions. 1986 Census.* Catalogue #94-120, Ottawa: Minister of Supply and Services Canada.

1988b   *Profiles Nova Scotia, Part 2: Census Divisions and Subdivisions. 1986 Census.* Catalogue #94-106 Ottawa: Minister of Supply and Services Canada.

1988c   *Profiles Quebec, Part 2, Volume 2 of 2: Census Divisions and Subdivisions. 1986 Census.* (Catalogue #94-110), Ottawa: Minister of Supply and Services Canada.

1988d   *Profiles — Urban and Rural Areas, Canada, Provinces and Territories Part 1, 1986* (Catalogue #94-129). Ottawa: Minister of Supply and Services Canada.

Statistics Canada. Housing, Family and Social Statistics Division
1990   *Immigrants in Canada. Selected Highlights.* Ottawa: Minister of Supply and Services Canada.

Stone, L. O., and S. Fletcher
1980   *A Profile of Canada's Older Population.* Montreal, Quebec: The Institute for Research on Public Policy.

Stones, M. J., A. Kozma, and L. Stones
1985   "Preliminary Findings on the Effects of Exercise Program Participation in Older Adults." *Canadian Journal of Public Health* 76: 272-273.

Storm, C., T. Storm, and J. Strike-Schurman
1985   "Obligations for Care: Beliefs in a Small Canadian Town." *Canadian Journal on Aging* 4(2): 75-85.

Strain, L. A.
1979   *Outdoor Recreation for Rural Senior Citizens.* Winnipeg, Manitoba: Natural Resources Institute, University of Manitoba.
Strain, L. A. , and N. L. Chappell
1982   "Outdoor Recreation and the Rural Elderly: Participation, Problems and Needs." *Therapeutic Recreation Journal* 16(4): 42-48.
Tefertiller, K.
1973   "Rural Development in an Urban Age." *American Journal of Agricultural Economics* 55(5), 771-777.
Thorne, S., C. Griffin, and M. Adlersberg
1986   "How's your Health?" *The Gerontion.* 1(5), 15-18.
Thurston, N. E., D. E. Larsen, A. W. Redemaker, and J. C. Kerr
1982   "Health Status of the Rural Elderly: A Picture of Health." Paper presented to the annual meeting of the Canadian Association on Gerontology , Winnipeg, Manitoba.
Torrance, G.
1987   "Socio-historical Overview: The Development of the Canadian Health System. in D. Coburn, C. D'Arcy, G. Torrance and P. New (eds.). *Health and Canadian Society. Sociological Perspectives.* Markham, Ontario: Fitzhenry and Whiteside.
Townsend, E., S. Anderson, and S. Jenner
1988   "Developing Rural Health Services: An Occupational Therapy Case Study." *Canadian Journal of Public Health* 79: 92-96.
Tuttle, P.
no date *Caregiver Support Demonstration Project.* Durham Regions Community Care Association. Whitby, Ontario.
Tyler, E. J.
1968   "The Farmer as a Social Class." In M. A. Tremblay, and W. J. Anderson (eds.). *Rural Canada in Transition: A Multidimensional Study of the Impact of Technology and Urbanization on Traditional Society.* Ottawa: Agricultural Economics Research Council. Pp. 228-340.
United Nations
1986   *Demographic Yearbook.* New York, NY: Department of Economic and Social Affairs, Statistical Office, United Nations.
Vanek, J.
1980   "Work, Leisure, and Family Roles: Farm Households in the United States, 1920-1955." *Journal of Family History* 5: 422-431.
Vester, N.
1982   *The Touch of Her Hand: Changing Role of Rural Women.* Edmonton, Alberta: Rural Education and Development Association.
Vivian, J. B.
1982   *Home Support Services Survey Project.* 2 vols. St. John's, Newfoundland: Newfoundland Department of Social Services.

Watkins, J. M., and D. A. Watkins
  1984   *Social Policy and the Rural Setting.* New York: Springer Publishing
          Company.
Weinert, C., and K. Long
  1987   "Understanding the Health Care Needs of Rural Families."
          Family Relations 36: 450-455.
Wenger, C.
  1982   "Ageing in Rural Communities: Family Contacts and Community
          Integration." *Ageing and Society* 2(2): 211-229.
  1986   "A Longitudinal Study of Changes and Adaptation in the Sup-
          port Networks of Welsh Elderly Over 75." *Journal of Cross Cul-
          tural Gerontology* 1(3): 277-304.
Whyte, D. R.
  1968   "Rural Canada in Transition." In M. A. Tremblay and W. J.
          Anderson (eds.). *Rural Canada in Transition: A Multidimensional
          Study of the Impact of Technology and Urbanization on Traditional
          Society.* Ottawa: Agricultural Economics Research Council. Pp.
          1-13.
Wilkening, E. A.
  1981   "Farm Families and Family Farming." In R. T. Coward and
          W. M. Smith, Jr. (eds.). *The Family in Rural Society: Westview
          Special Studies in Contemporary Social Issues.* Boulder, Colorado:
          Westview Press. Pp. 27-36.
Wilkins, R., and O. Adams.
  1987   "Health Expectancy in Canada, Late 1970s: Demographic, Re-
          gional and Social Dimensions." In D. Coburn, C. D'Arcy,
          G. Torrance and P. New (eds.). *Health and Canadian Society. So-
          ciological Perspectives.* Markham Ontario: Fitzhenry and
          Whiteside. Pp.36-56.
Wilson, C. R.
  1986   "The Plains — A Regional Overview." In R. Morrison and C. R.
          Wilson (eds.). *Native Peoples: The Canadian Experience.* Toronto:
          McClelland and Stewart. Pp. 353-357.
Windley, P. G., and R. Scheidt
  1983   "Service Utilization and Activity Participations Among Psycho-
          logically Vulnerable and Well Elderly in Rural Small Towns."
          The Gerontologist 23(3): 283-287.
  1988   "Rural Small Towns: An Environmental Context for Aging."
          Journal of Rural Studies 4(2): 151-158.
Wister, A.
  1985   "Living Arrangement Choices Among the Elderly." *Canadian
          Journal on Aging* 4(3): 127-144.
Wolfe, R. and R. Nutter
  1986   "Project Involvement. Community Work with Seniors in Alberta.

Volume II. Technical Report." Edmonton, Alberta: Alberta Council on Aging.

Wood, L.
1981   "Loneliness and Life Satisfaction among the Rural Elderly." Paper presented to the annual meeting of the Canadian Association on Gerontology, Toronto, Ontario.

Youmans, E.
1967   *Older Rural Americans: A Sociological Perspective.* Lexington: University of Kentucky Press.

Young, T.
1987   "The Health of Indians in Northwestern Ontario: A Historical Perspective." In D. Coburn, C. D'Arcy, G. Torrance and P. New (eds). *Health and Canadian Society. Sociological Perspectives.* Fitzhenry and Whiteside. Pp.109-125.

Zarit, S., N. Orr, and J. Zarit
1985.   *The Hidden Victims of Alzheimer's Disease: Families Under Stress.* New York, New York University Press.

Zarit, S. Reever, K. and J. Bach-Peterson
1980   "Relatives of the Impaired Elderly: Correlates of Feelings of Burden." *The Gerontologist* 20: 649-655.

Zuzanek, J. and R. Mannell
1983   "Work-leisure Relationships from a Sociological and Social Psychological Perspective." *Leisure Studies* 2: 327-344.

INDEX